The Golfer's Companion

THE GOLFER'S COMPANION

JAMES A. FRANK
Editor, *GOLF Magazine*

KEY PORTER BOOKS

To Belle, Willy, and Rebecca —
the rest of my foursome

Canadian Cataloguing in Publication Data

Frank, James A.
   The golfer's companion

ISBN 1-55013-395-0

1. Golf. I. Title.

GV965.F73 1992   796.352   C91-095639-1

Key Porter Books Limited
70 The Esplanade
Toronto, Ontario
Canada M5E 1R2

Distributed in the United States of America by:
Publishers Group West
4065 Hollis
Emeryville, CA 94608

Design: Scott Richardson
Typesetting: Compeer Typographic Services Limited

Printed and bound in China

92 93 94 95 96 6 5 4 3 2 1

◀ **From the mountains sur-
rounding Banff Springs
Golf Club, Alberta, to
the desert floor, nature is
the ultimate golf course
architect.**

Contents

Introduction

This is not a book of golf instruction.

Stores are full of how-to manuals "written" by famous golf pros revealing their secrets for longer drives, straighter putts, closer chips, lower punches, higher lobs, and so on. If you're like me, your bookshelves already overflow with more advice than one person can absorb —let alone put into practice—in a single lifetime.

So, there's no instruction here. Instead, this book is intended to be a source of inspiration.

No, you won't find any motivational speeches or prayers to the golf gods. You will, however, learn a little history and uncover some of the game's traditions. I hope you'll be encouraged while reading about the great players and courses—and amused by some of the game's tribal rituals.

Unlike taking an overlap grip or setting up for a controlled fade, there are no right and wrong ways to use this book. You might start by dipping into the chapter on history and wondering for yourself where golf really came from.

Does anyone remember when clubs were called "mashies" and "spoons"? Equipment has evolved and revolved since balls were leather sacks stuffed with feathers, and clubs were handmade. Every change had great effect, both on the players and on the game itself.

Looking for a good course? You'll find one made up of eighteen great holes, which, if you could play it, would provide more than enough track for even the top pros. Every hole presents both a mental and a physical challenge. No doubt you'll recognize many of the holes from television. You even may have played a few. (If so, did you play them the way the architects intended?)

Even in his eighties, American golf great Sam Snead is still going strong.

Ireland's beautiful Waterville links is open to all.

7

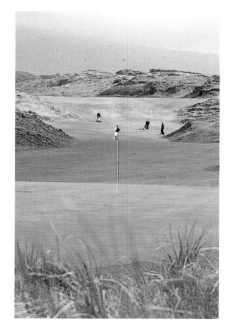

A late nineteenth-century etching of an English women's golf club.

Nineteenth-century players at a course in Wimbledon, England.

Because golf is only as good as the people who play it, I have included biographies of twenty-nine superstars whose careers span more than one hundred years. All these greats possessed (and in some cases still possess) both the game and the mind to tackle the toughest courses and opponents. See if you agree with the selections in this very subjective hall of fame.

There are also lists of tournament winners and money records included to refresh your memory — and maybe win you a few wagers at the nineteenth hole. Finally, there are pages for entering your own scores, which may be as memorable to you as some of history's other notable rounds, such as Tom Watson's 66 (to Jack Nicklaus's 67) at Turnberry in 1977, Johnny Miller's 63 at Oakmont in 1973, and Sam Snead's 66 in 1979 — shot when he was sixty-seven!

This book won't tell you how to play the game any better, but I do hope it will help you enjoy the game more.

Nearly every history of golf begins with the observation that if you give a man a stick, he'll try to hit something with it. There must be some truth to that because numerous countries offer evidence of early ball-and-stick games. But that doesn't give any one of them the rightful claim to be the birthplace of golf.

The ancient Romans played something called *paganica* when they conquered Britain (try calling your next opponent a ''pagan'' and see what kind of response you get). The Dutch played *kolven* and *colf* as far back as the thirteenth century. The French and Italians had *jeu de mail* and *pall mall* in the early seventeenth century. Even the Chinese recently put in a bid, saying their *chuiwan* dates back to A.D. 943.

Good for them. But none were golf.

What we call golf originated in Scotland. True, there was significant commerce between the port cities of eastern Scotland and Holland, with records of balls and clubs being traded back and forth. Nevertheless, it was the Scots who thought of using different clubs for different shots, and who decided the ball should finish in a hole rather than banging up against a church door.

The first record of golf in Scotland hails from 1457. The Scots and the English were on only slightly worse terms than they are today, so King James II of Scotland issued a proclamation forbidding the playing of ''gowf'' and ''futeball'' because they were cutting into his soldiers' archery practice. When peace came in 1503, Scotland's James IV took up the game: the account books of the royal court note purchases of clubs and balls, as well as the settling of a golf bet (the King lost).

The Old Course at St. Andrews, Scotland, has been in play for more than four hundred years.

Let the Game Begin

Although only 305 yards long, the 10th hole at Royal Melbourne, one of Australia's top courses, is no pushover.

The procession of the Silver Club at the Honourable Company of Edinburgh Golfers in the late eighteenth century.

Mary, Queen of Scots, may have been the first female golfer. In 1567, she was spotted on the course a few days after the mysterious death of her husband, Lord Darnley. This indiscretion cost Mary her chance to play—as well as her crown, and eventually her head.

After Scotland and England united in 1603, golf crossed the border and became a favorite of the English kings. In 1604, a royal clubmaker was appointed, and soon a seven-hole course was laid out near London, on the Black Heath by the River Thames. Nearly four hundred years later, the Royal Blackheath Golf Club still sits on the same venerable land, although a ''club'' wasn't established there until 1766.

By the late 1600s, golf was enjoyed almost exclusively by the well-to-do, for they were the only ones with the necessary time and money. Two areas of eastern Scotland were renowned for golf: north of Edinburgh, on the Links of Leith, and across the Firth of Forth, at St. Andrews, on the North Sea. In both cases, play was over ''links land,'' the sandy, grassy area between the water and the mainland. It was on these ''links'' that men—and golf was solely a man's game—gathered to play and socialize.

Clubs formed in the eighteenth century, usually around existing orders of Freemasons. Many of the traditions associated with golf clubs today—secret votes, ''blackballing'' candidates for membership, special crests and clothing—originated with these societies of wealthy Scottish and English gentlemen.

In the early days, golf was almost an afterthought for the Freemasons, who were more interested in eating and drinking. They also were very secretive, often

Mary, Queen of Scots, play-ing golf at St. Andrews.

destroying rather than saving club records. The penchant for privacy among these orders has hindered chroniclers of golf history. What records do remain note enormous feasts of fowl, beef, seafood, whisky, and wine; golf was a means of working up an appetite before the meal.

In time, being a Freemason proved not as much fun as being a golfer, and true golf clubs were established. In 1744, the Honourable Company of Edinburgh Golfers was formed, with play over the five-hole Links of Leith. This club was only one of several using Leith, but in time it became the most famous. Today, although the club's official name remains the same, its home is Muir-field, the spectacular course an hour east of Edinburgh.

Soon after the founding of the Honourable Company, the Edinburgh Town Council presented the members with a silver club and the idea of holding a competition for it. John Rattray won what seems to be the world's first club championship, and was named captain of the Company. Members have been playing for the Silver Club ever since.

Charles I receives news of
the outbreak of the Irish
Rebellion while playing golf
on the Links of Leith.

With competition came a need for rules. In its first year, the Honourable Company adopted thirteen rules of play, just enough to fill one side of a piece of paper. (Compare that to the 120-page book we now follow.) The original rules managed a somewhat different game from what we know today, but with much the same spirit and intent.

Rule number 3, for example, read: "You are not to Change the Ball which you Strike off the Tee." Number 12: "He, Whose Ball lyes furthest from the hole is Obliged to play first." Other rules forbid moving "Stones, Bones . . . for the Sake of playing your Ball" and decree that "the Ball so Stop'd Must be played where it lyes," even if "stop'd" by horse or dog.

On May 14, 1754, "twenty-two Noblemen and Gentlemen being admirers of the ancient and healthfull exercise of the Golf" met to form the Society of St. Andrews Golfers in the small university and cathedral town. The naturally formed links land at St. Andrews was well known to Scottish golfers, including those from Leith. When the St. Andrews club was formed, the Honourable Company's rules were adopted with little variation.

The two clubs shared other traditions as well. Since holes were routed over public land where people gathered, golfers needed some way to give warning that they were playing through. A bright red coat, they figured, would be easily seen and force others to stand clear. (Remember, it was the upper classes playing, the lower classes out strolling.) The bright costume also suited the clubs' origins in Freemasonry; the secret societies were fond of fancy regalia. Soon each club adopted a uniform. Both St. Andrews and the Honourable Company chose red coats, with different colors for hats, buttons, and insignia. (Annual meetings at St. Andrews are still attended by members in bright red waistcoats.)

The original St. Andrews course was twelve holes, then eleven. The skinny sliver of land along St. Andrews Bay didn't have room for adjacent holes, so golfers played out and in over the same ground, creating a ''round''of twenty-two holes. In 1764, the first four holes were reworked into two, trimming the course to eighteen. In time, some greens were enlarged so that two holes — one going out, the other coming in—would end on the same putting surface (but with different flags and cups). The course as we know it today was in play by the early 1840s.

Soon after St. Andrews went to eighteen holes, that became the standard. In 1893, the course cut its cups at 4¼ inches in diameter and that too became the norm (before then, the size was random, based on who and what was doing the cutting). How did St. Andrews eclipse the older Honourable Company as the game's trendsetter?

The Edinburgh Golfers changed courses a few times, moving east from Leith to Musselburgh in 1836, then to Muirfield in 1891. During those periods of homelessness, their influence diminished. But, more importantly, in 1834, King William IV was inveigled into granting St. Andrews a ''royal'' designation. The Royal and Ancient Golf Club of St. Andrews had acquired its full name — and full power.

Golf remained a rich man's game until the mid-1800s, even though most links were open to all. With the creation of a cheaper, more resilient golf ball — made of gutta-percha, a sap-like substance from the sapodilla trees of Malaysia — the game became affordable for the middle class.

While golf was growing in popularity at home, the soldiers and merchants of the British Empire were spreading the gospel. A club was formed in Calcutta in 1829, and in Bombay in 1842; Australia's Royal Adelaide Club was established in 1871, Royal Melbourne in 1891; Cape Golf Course, South Africa, opened in 1885. Even Buenos Aires had a course in 1878, constructed by British engineers who were in Argentina to build a railroad. Courses also appeared in Thailand, Hong Kong, and Malaya.

In North America, the oldest continuous club is the Royal Montreal Golf Club, which opened in 1873. The Royal Quebec Golf Club followed in 1875, then the Toronto Golf Club in 1876. It would be another twelve years before golf was officially established in the United States.

Prestwick, on Scotland's west coast, opened in 1851 and hosted the first ''Open'' championship on October

17, 1860. Actually, it wasn't that open, as only eight pros played. Willie Park of Musselburgh was the winner, going around the twelve-hole, 3,803-yard circuit three times in 174 strokes — 42 over par. Park didn't collect any money, but was presented with the Championship Challenge Belt, made of red Morocco leather and silver. (He and his brothers, also professionals, did parlay the success into big-stakes matches against wealthy amateurs and other pros.) At Prestwick again, in 1861, the Open became truly open when all the country's top players were invited. Old Tom Morris, the pro at Prestwick, won the first of his four Open titles, a feat that would be equalled by his son, Young Tom.

The Open remained at Prestwick until 1872, after which it alternated with St. Andrews and Musselburgh. In 1892, Muirfield hosted its first Open, one year after the Honourable Company moved there. Today, the British Open rota consists of St. Andrews, Muirfield, Troon, and Turnberry in Scotland, and St. George's, Birkdale, and Lytham and St. Annes in England — all seaside courses, in keeping with tradition.

Golf in Britain had mushroomed. In 1850, there were 17 golf societies. By 1890 the number had grown to 387, playing over 140 courses. By 1990, there were nearly 2,500 courses in the British Isles.

Just as phenomenal was the growth of the game in the United States. The British had exported golf to the Colonies in the 1700s: there are scanty records of a golf club in Charleston, South Carolina, in 1743, and another in Savannah, Georgia, in 1795. Then the game died out, not to return until the 1880s. There may have been occurrences in the meantime, perhaps drifting down from Canada, but most historians date golf's birth in America at 1888.

The progenitor was one John Reid, a Scottish (of course) merchant living north of New York City. He asked a friend traveling to Scotland to purchase clubs and balls from the shop of Old Tom Morris, back in his native St. Andrews. On February 22, 1888, Reid and five friends tested the equipment in a cow pasture in Yonkers, New York. They played all that summer, and at the end of the year formed the St. Andrew's (with an apostrophe, in deference to the original) Golf Club.

The course moved twice before settling on its current site in Hastings, New York, in 1897. Meanwhile, Scottish pros had begun crossing the Atlantic to design courses, manufacture equipment, and teach rich Americans the game. Willie Dunn of Musselburgh came to America in 1890 and laid out Shinnecock Hills on the links-like land of Long Island; this club built America's first clubhouse.

The first eighteen-hole layout in the United States, the Chicago Golf Club, opened in 1893. It was designed by American Charles Blair Macdonald, who had attended college in St. Andrews, where he had fallen in love with the game. Upon returning to the American heartland, he introduced others to golf and designed a few small courses. During his lifetime, Macdonald designed more courses, was involved in the formation of the United States Golf Association (USGA), and won the first ''official'' U.S. Amateur, in 1895. He was America's first golf nut.

How did golf grow in America? In 1888, there was

one course—Reid's six-holer in Yonkers. By 1896, there were more than 80; by 1900, the number was 982; and in 1990, nearly 13,000.

In December 1894, the USGA was established to govern and nurture the game in the United States. The following October, the first Amateur was held at the Newport Golf Club in Rhode Island, one of the USGA's five founding clubs (along with St. Andrew's, Chicago, Shinnecock Hills, and The Country Club outside Boston). The first U.S. Open was played on the same course the next day. Ten pros and one amateur competed, with the tournament won by the twenty-one-year-old assistant at Newport, Englishman Horace Rawlins. His one-day score of 91–82/173 earned him a $50 gold medal and $150 in cash.

Medal Day in the late 1800s at the Royal Blackheath Golf Club, London, England.

On the European continent, the first course was established at Pau, France, in 1856 (supposedly at the suggestion of Scottish soldiers convalescing after fighting Napoleon in Spain), then golf came to the Iberian Peninsula in 1889, when English vacationers opened a course on the Portuguese coast. Today, from Scandinavia to the Mediterranean, courses are sprouting and new disciples signing on.

In Japan, a layout was built on the slopes of Mount Kobe in 1903; today, the Japanese are avid golfers, although a lack of land makes new courses prohibitively expensive to build and clubs to join.

The first women's club opened at St. Andrews in 1867, no doubt spinning the vehemently anti-female Freemasons in their graves. The first British Ladies' Amateur was held in 1893, and the first U.S. Women's Amateur in 1895, the same year as the men's inaugural event. But there was no U.S. Women's Open until 1946, and no Ladies' British Open until 1976.

Britain's best dominated the game through the turn of the century, led by the ''Great Triumvirate'' of Harry Vardon, John H. Taylor, and James Braid, who won sixteen British Opens among them from 1894 to 1914. The first home-grown pro to win the U.S. Open was Johnny McDermott in 1911 (he won again in 1912), but it took the 1913 victory by twenty-year-old unknown Francis Ouimet over Vardon and fellow Briton Ted Ray to excite the American public.

In the 1920s, American pros came into their own, led by the likes of Walter Hagen and Gene Sarazen. Their success paved the way for future American pros

such as Sam Snead, Byron Nelson, and Ben Hogan, who led in turn to Arnold Palmer, Jack Nicklaus, Tom Watson, and today's shotmaking superstars.

Before the pros took over the game for good, however, it was an American amateur, Bobby Jones, who bridged the gap between golf's two leading lands. Jones triumphed on both sides of the Atlantic, climaxing with his Grand Slam in 1930—the U.S. and British Open and Amateur titles. Jones represented all that was good about the game, and he was as big a hero in Britain as he was at home.

In Bobby Jones, America gave something back to the British, who had given the game to America and the world. After nearly five hundred years, golf had come full circle.

Harry Vardon, Francis Ouimet and Ted Ray at the 1913 U.S. Open.

Today's golfer hears the term "game improvement" and thinks it applies only to equipment introduced during the last two decades, particularly balls that fly farther and last longer, and clubs that make bad shots acceptable (maybe even good). However, as long as there has been golf equipment, there have been game improvement features. Nearly every important change in clubs and balls has made golf easier, cheaper, and more accessible to more players, resulting in the game's rapid growth.

The first improvement came sometime in the late seventeenth century with the invention of the feathery ball, a small leather sack stuffed with a top-hat's worth of goose feathers. This ball flew much farther than the wooden ones it replaced. But feather-stuffing was done by hand, and since it took one man a full day to make four balls, they were expensive. The feathery also was easily ruined, especially when wet. To lessen the damage, the clubheads of the day were made of soft wood, cut in long, banana-like shapes. Because irons could destroy a ball with one blow, they were used sparingly, usually to dig the ball out of wagon ruts and other inhospitable lies.

Golf made a quantum leap around 1850 with the development of the gutta-percha ball. After the expensive feathery, the "gutty" was a bargain. The balls were cheaply and easily made by cutting chunks of the semi-hardened sap, then rounding them by hand or mold. The gutty lasted longer, flew farther, and rolled truer than the feathery, and if damaged, needed only a whack with a hammer or a run through a ball press to put it right. (Gutties tended to break apart, sometimes in flight. Players were allowed to drop a new ball on the spot where the largest piece of the old ball landed.)

Clubs and
Balls: Getting
Better All
the Time

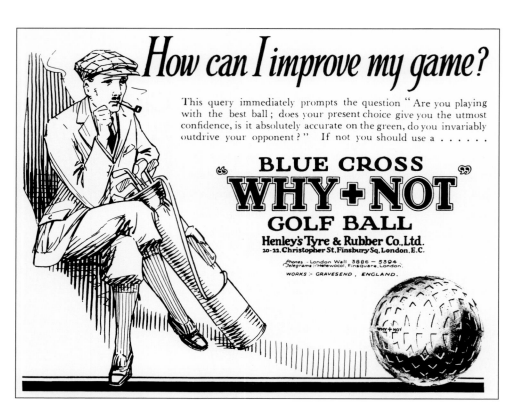

Because the gutty flew farther, hole yardage had to be increased; and because the ball was cheap, the game boomed, and courses had to allow for more players. Around 1857, the Old Course at St. Andrews (then the only course at St. Andrews) was widened to welcome more players.

The gutty also had an effect on clubs. To accommodate the softer ball, hardwood heads became shorter and squatter and were fitted with inserts, usually leather, for the first time. This era also saw hickory become the choice in golf shafts. But, most significantly, irons came into their own because, unlike the feathery, the gutty could withstand an iron's blows (and, if not, the ball could always be remolded). Young Tom Morris was one of the first to prove that irons could be used effectively:

he won four British Opens in a row from 1868 to 1872 (the Open was not held in 1871 because Young Tom had been given permanent custody of the championship belt in 1870 and a new prize had not yet been decided upon).

In time, golfers noticed that the nicks, scratches, and gouges made by clubs actually improved the ball's performance, resulting in longer, straighter shots. Soon balls were being scored during manufacture, often with intricate patterns. One popular design was a raised bramble pattern. The ''dimple'' wasn't patented until 1905.

After golf came to America in 1888, the United States soon became the world leader in designing and manufacturing equipment. A.G. Spalding, which made its name making baseballs, was the first company to assemble and sell clubs in the United States, in the early 1890s. One of the more innovative firms was the now-defunct BGI, which built clubs based on its expertise with firearms (BGI stood for Bridgeport Gun Implement). Burke Golf Company supplied wood for buggy whips until someone noticed that horseless carriages didn't respond to whips; Burke became a leading maker of hickory shafts, then finished clubs. MacGregor's roots were in the shoe business; one of its craftsmen fashioned the first persimmon club from the wood used to make lasts for children's shoes.

The most important innovation of the day was the first wound golf ball, introduced in 1898. Invented by an entrepreneur from Cleveland, Ohio, named Coburn Haskell, it featured a small rubber core wrapped with continuous rubber windings and encased in a thin gutta-percha cover. The new ball flew and rolled farther than any before it and was easier to control.

Long-nosed wooden clubs like this "green putter" were used from the fifteenth century to the mid-1800s.

Two turn-of-the-century balls show some of the variety in cover designs invented over the years.

Like the gutty fifty years earlier, the Haskell revolutionized the game. The inventor persuaded a leading British player, John H. Taylor, to give the ball a try. Never a long hitter, Taylor teed off on the first hole at New York's Rockaway Hunting Club, figuring the group on the green 250 yards away was safe. His drive rolled up to the players as they were holing out.

In 1901, Walter Travis won his second consecutive U.S. Amateur with the Haskell. In 1902, the British Open fell to Alexander Herd, whose use of the Haskell won the ball acceptance overseas. The era of the wound ball, the predecessor of the modern three-piece ball, had begun.

As usual, a new ball meant new clubs. Harder-faced woods were needed for the softer wound ball, and persimmon fit the bill (as did woods made of laminated maple, which appeared in the 1940s). Hard inserts in the face became standard in woods, while iron heads were enlarged to keep the ball on the face longer for control.

The success of the Haskell led to further experimentation. Balata, a natural rubber, became the cover of choice, replacing gutta-percha. Some companies tinkered with the hollow rubber core, filling it with all manner of substances trying to achieve the perfect weight. Among those attempted were lead, glue, honey, even tapioca. (Modern hollow-core balls use water and salts.) The company that manufactured the original Haskell, tire manufacturer B.F. Goodrich, mixed technologies and produced a "pneumatic" golf ball filled with air. Although it flew a long way, the ball sometimes exploded in flight or in a pocket. In the 1907 U.S. Open, Alex Campbell was on the edge of a green in two, twenty feet from the hole. He took four to get down, his Pneumatic literally having lost its breath.

Progress with balls led to new rules. The two rulemaking bodies, the Royal and Ancient Golf Club of St. Andrews and the USGA, took years to agree on guidelines for ball size and weight. In 1932, the USGA settled on a weight of 1.62 ounces and a diameter of 1.68 inches. Eventually the British went along, and those specifications remain today.

In turn, rule changes influenced equipment. Steel shafts were ruled legal in 1926 and made hickories all but obsolete within a decade — although Bobby Jones won his Grand Slam of 1930 with hickory-shafted clubs.

In the 1920s, a battle raged over face grooves on clubs. Scotsman Jock Hutchison won the 1921 British Open using irons with deep grooves. Face markings were a recent invention, coming after turn-of-the-century players noticed that roughing up their traditionally smooth-faced irons put more spin on the ball. Punch dots were the first manufactured markings, followed by patterns of dots, dashes, shallow grooves, and then Hutchison's deep grooves. Deep grooves were banned shortly after his victory, and regulations on groove size followed soon after.

As equipment proliferated, so did accessories. The golf bag made its first commercial appearance around 1891 in England. Called a ''carrier,'' it usually came equipped with a stake or an arrangement of legs that allowed it to stand on its own. The first ball ''pick-ups,'' forerunners of the shag bag, also were patented in the early 1890s, as were gadgets such as the tethered practice ball, hand-held ball cleaner, and adjustable-headed club.

This 1897 long iron featured a wooden insert.

In 1848, the introduction of the cheaper, more resilient gutta percha ball made the game more accessible for the middle class.

The tee has a history, too. Players used to take a pinch of sand and dab of water and mold a tiny mound for the ball with their fingers. Tees were marketed as early as the 1890s, but the one that caught on was the Wooden Reddy Tee, invented in 1920 by William Lowell, a New Jersey dentist. Its success was assured when F. W. Woolworth, the dime-store chain, placed a huge order, and Walter Hagen was sufficiently impressed with the product to place one behind his ear as he strode the fairways.

While new products made golf better and easier, some of the romance of the old days was disappearing. For centuries, clubs had been known by name, usually Scottish terms that described their shape or use. As clubs became more uniform and reliable, use of those names faded away. They're worth remembering here (with their closest modern equivalents).

The "driver" was the club that "drove" the ball into play off the tee. The "brassie" (2-wood) had a brass plate on its sole. The curved face of the "spoon" (3-wood) made it resemble a piece of silverware; in fact, "spoon" was used to describe woods as far back as the 1700s. "Cleek" (4-wood) referred to a Scottish walking stick that was hooked at the end, while "baffy" (5-wood) took its name from "baff," meaning a "blow made by something soft."

Irons also had names. "Mashies," today's long irons, derived from the Scottish word for sledgehammer. "Niblick" meaning "short-nosed," was attached first to early woods, then the irons used to get the ball in the air, especially from wagon ruts and other tracks. There were also spade mashies, mashie niblicks, and other compound names for clubs with different lofts and applications.

These titles vanished by the late 1930s when steel shafts and other advancements led to the creation of the "matched set." Quality was high, but quaintness was lost as each club became known by number.

In the 1930s, companies hired advisory staffs of top pros to help design and promote products. After Bobby Jones retired from competitive play, he became an adviser to (and board member of) Spalding. Wilson Sporting Goods, which listed Sam Snead and Babe Zaharias among its staff players, had its roots in a Chicago meat-packing firm that made tennis-racquet strings out of animal entrails. One of the company's first big golf products was the sand wedge, designed by Gene Sarazen to remedy his own problems getting out of bunkers.

Golf boomed after the Second World War. Pros such as Ben Hogan and Arnold Palmer entered the club business, as did a host of small firms that made precision parts for the growing aerospace industry. As they worked with new techniques of molding metal, an old idea for redistributing the weight of an iron head was put into practice. By moving the weight away from the small sweet spot in the center of the face, and creating a cavity on the back side, shots hit high or low on the clubface or off the heel or toe would still fly far and relatively straight. That game-improvement idea was the beginning of cavity-back (perimeter-weighted) irons.

In the mid-1960s, cavity-backs challenged traditional forged irons. Karsten Solheim, creator of Ping clubs, said that he initially placed a piece of metal over the hollow area on his new irons because he thought customers weren't ready for the new look; but once golfers hit the clubs, he reported, it didn't matter what they looked like, they sold!

By the 1970s, the same investment-casting processes that made the new irons were used to create metal woods. Again, the weight was moved out to the edges of the head for more solid, dependable shots off mishits.

By the late 1980s, metal woods and cavity-back irons were the most popular clubs in their categories. Golfers at all levels found that they could buy a better game — which is much easier than practicing. And as earlier advances had done, these products of progress opened golf's doors to more and more eager participants.

About seventy years after Coburn Haskell changed golf forever with his three-piece ball, Spalding unveiled a two-piece ball, a solid mass in a tough, synthetic cover.

It was an immediate success, promising more distance and a longer life. True, the early Top-Flite and other two-piecers felt as hard as rocks, but since the days of the gutty, golfers have flocked to any ball that gives them both length and durability.

New covers, cores, and aerodynamically advanced dimples make balls better and better. New ideas in clubs keep coming along as well. In the last few years, bold claims have been made for graphite and other exotic materials, irons that are forged to look like cavity-backs, clubs specifically for seniors and women, and the latest —jumbo-size woods.

One of the best of today's superstars, England's Nick Faldo, can still have fun on the course.

Who is a great golfer? Where you play, it might be the club champion or the old geezer who cleans up on the final hole. Maybe greatness is the woman with the perfect putting stroke or the young pup on tour currently beating up on the big boys. All these players are great — within their circles and over a defined period of time. But truly "great"?

In pulling together a list of twenty-nine "great" golfers, the principal criterion, naturally, is winning, but not simply as the result of good ball-striking. I wanted players who will be praised long after their glory days are past. Those who achieved fame for the game as well as for themselves. Golfers who left a mark.

Perhaps they set a record for tournament victories, or developed a swing that others rushed to copy. Maybe their greatness comes from "fire in the belly" or "grace under pressure." "Great" certainly means domination, as exemplified by Jack Nicklaus, Ben Hogan, Byron Nelson, and Mickey Wright, all of whom were easy picks. Then there were the hard ones, some of whom may not make your list.

All twenty-nine, though, possess some of the qualities expressed above. And they all fit early British golf writer Bernard Darwin's description of another uncontestable on my list—Harry Vardon: "He did what only a very great player can do; he raised the general conception of what was possible in his game and forced his nearest rivals to attain a higher standard by attempting that which they would otherwise have deemed impossible."

That's what makes a winning—and a great—golfer.

Players of Note

Isao Aoki, from Akibo, Japan, was the first from his country to succeed on the international golf scene. After developing a distinctive short, choppy swing, and a unique style of putting, with the toe of the putter well off the ground, Aoki turned pro in 1964 and notched his first victory seven years later. Since then, he's scored more than fifty wins in Japan, topping that tour's money list five times. In 1983 and '87 he captured the Japan Open. He also owns significant world titles, including the 1978 World Match Play and 1983 European Open. Aoki is best remembered in the West for battling Jack Nicklaus to the wire in a losing effort at the 1980 U.S. Open, and for holing out from 130 yards on the final hole to win the 1983 Hawaiian Open.

Isao Aoki

Japan
b. 1942
World Match Play, 1978
European Open, 1983
Japan Open, 1983, 1987

He was called the "Silver Scot" for his country of birth and elegant gray hair, yet Tommy Armour achieved fame and fortune in the United States. He came to America after serving during the First World War, where he lost an eye but picked up metal plates in his head and left arm. The hallmark of Armour's game was deadly accurate iron play, which he used to good advantage in 1927, winning his first major tournament, the U.S. Open at Oakmont Country Club. In 1930, he topped Gene Sarazen for the PGA Championship, and the next year captured the British Open at Carnoustie. After cutting back on playing, Armour became a highly sought-after teacher and the author of two bestsellers—*How to Play Your Best Golf All the Time* and *A Round of Golf with Tommy Armour*.

Tommy Armour

Scotland/United States
1895–1968
U.S. Open, 1927
PGA Championship, 1930
British Open, 1931
Canadian Open, 1927, 1930, 1934

Seve Ballesteros

Spain
b. 1957
Masters, 1980, 1983
British Open, 1979, 1984,
1988

Crowd-pleaser Severiano Ballesteros grew up in northern Spain, knocking balls around the fields with a castoff 3-iron. The lack of equipment helped him develop a remarkable imagination for shotmaking, which he has needed because his game can be as unpredictable as his moods. He burst upon the scene in 1976 at the British Open at Royal Birkdale, where he finished tied for second. As well as topping the money list and recording his first victory, Ballesteros finished the season the youngest golfer to win the European Tour's award for low scoring average. Since then, he has won many events worldwide, including two Masters and three British Opens. He has also compiled a strong Ryder Cup record — playing on every European squad but one since 1979.

Henry Cotton

England
1907–1987
British Open, 1934, 1937,
1948

English-born Henry Cotton was little known outside Europe during his playing heydey, the '30s, but he proved influential over time. He was one of the first professionals to come from the outside; that is, he didn't begin as a caddie or a pro's son. Perhaps to overcome this, Cotton practiced religiously — between rounds, even between tournaments, which was almost unheard of at the time. His hard work paid off, producing pinpoint accuracy from tee to green, and victories in Britain and on the continent during the early '30s. But he needed a British Open to establish himself. He eventually won three—1934, '37, and '48. After his playing days passed, Cotton gained new fame as a teacher, author, and course designer.

As the '90s begin, the dominant player in golf is Englishman Nick Faldo, who turned pro at age nineteen. Like his game, his progress has been slow and steady. In 1987 he won the British Open at Muirfield with a final round of eighteen pars. Since then, practice, perseverance, and a revamped swing have pushed him over the top. In the twelve majors after Muirfield, he notched three victories (the 1989 and '90 Masters, and 1990 British Open), a second, two thirds, and a fourth. Although not flashy, he doesn't shrink from challenge. Paired with Greg Norman in the third round of the 1990 British Open at St. Andrews, Faldo easily won their "match," 67–76. He won the Open by five shots the next day, proving his championship mettle.

Nick Faldo

England
b. 1957
Masters, 1989, 1990
British Open, 1987, 1990

It will be a long time before we see a golfer more exciting than Walter Hagen. The "Haig" won countless tournaments, but it is his major record that excels: four British Opens (1922, '24, '28, '29), two U.S. Opens ('14 and '19), and five PGA Championships ('21, then four in a row starting in 1924). Hagen was the first American to make a living solely from golf, yet thought nothing of blowing the winner's check in a single night. Even his swing mirrored the devil-may-care '20s, a swaying lunge that often left him in trouble. Inspired shotmaking, and clever comments and ploys that kept opponents off-balance, usually saved him. Eventually, the good life eroded his skills. It never diminished his style.

Walter Hagen

United States
1892–1969
U.S. Open, 1914, 1919
PGA Championship, 1921,
1924, 1925, 1926, 1927
British Open, 1922, 1924,
1928, 1929
Canadian Open, 1931

Ben Hogan

United States
b. 1912
U.S. Open, 1948, 1950, 1951, 1953
PGA Championship, 1946, 1948
Masters, 1951, 1953
British Open, 1953

Ben Hogan, perhaps the best ball-striker of all, struggled for years before achieving greatness. He turned pro in 1931, but it wasn't until he transformed his swing in the late '40s that he blossomed, winning the 1946 and '48 PGA Championship and 1948 U.S. Open. Having finally made it, he nearly lost it all in a head-on collision with a bus, but determination and resolve powered a remarkable comeback. Little more than a year after the accident, he won the 1950 U.S. Open. The next year he captured his first Masters and another Open, and, in 1953, a small slam — the Masters and U.S. and British opens. In the '50s, Hogan launched an equipment company, dedicating himself to club manufacture as he had to his playing.

Robert Tyre Jones, Jr.

United States
1902–1971
U.S. Open, 1923, 1926, 1929, 1930
British Open, 1926, 1927, 1930
United States Amateur, 1924, 1925, 1927, 1928, 1930
British Amateur, 1930

Bobby Jones was the best of his era, yet he played tournament golf for only fifteen years, beginning at age fourteen. He played just a few months a year, when he wasn't in school or, later, practicing law in his native Atlanta. But most surprisingly, Jones never turned professional. Golf was his game, not his life. Between 1922 and 1930, he won four U.S. Opens, five U.S. Amateurs, and three British Opens. His crowning achievement was capturing the ''Grand Slam'' in 1930 — the U.S. and British Open and Amateur championships. Immediately afterward, he retired from competitive golf to concentrate on instructional films, books, and golf equipment. And, he founded and designed Augusta National Golf Club, home of The Masters. It is a fitting memorial.

The leading Canadian golfer of the 1960s and '70s was George Knudson. Possessing a smooth, almost effortless swing, Knudson played on the U.S. tour from 1961 to 1972, where he was a consistent money-earner and occasional champion, recording eight career victories. After two wins on the American tour in 1968, Knudson spent most of his time in Canada. He was a familiar presence in national events, notably the Canadian PGA, which he won five times between 1964 and 1977. He also played for his country in the World Cup, taking individual honors in 1966 and teaming with Al Balding to bring home the trophy in 1968. His best showing in a major was the 1969 Masters, where he finished tied for second, one stroke behind George Archer.

George Knudson

Canada
1937–1989
World Cup individual title, 1966
World Cup team title, 1968

Bobby Locke proved that an unorthodox style can pay off. He played every shot to move sharply right to left; he even hooked his putts, yet he was brilliant on the greens. After dominating events in his native South Africa, Locke left home in 1936, looking for stiffer competition. He played around the world with great success, winning more than eighty tournaments, including four British Opens (1949, '50, '52, '57). Although he won six U.S. events and finished second in earnings in 1947, he was snubbed by jealous American pros. In 1949, they found a way to ban him for a small infraction. Tour officials later apologized, but Locke never returned. Instead, the rest of the world got to see one of golf's more interesting players.

Bobby Locke

South Africa
1917–1987
British Open, 1949, 1950, 1952, 1957
Canadian Open, 1947

Nancy Lopez

United States

b. 1957

LPGA Championship, 1978, 1985, 1989

"Nancy with the smiling eyes" came along just when the Ladies' Professional Golf Association needed a star. After turning pro in 1977, she captured the public's attention by winning nine tournaments, including five in a row, in 1978. Mixing long, straight drives with eagle-eye putting, she maintained her hot streak in 1979, with eight more titles. Although her winning ways cooled down somewhat in the '80s, in 1983 Lopez became the youngest player, male or female, to earn more than $1 million. In 1987, she took her 35th title and gained automatic admission to the exclusive LPGA Hall of Fame. Today a lighter schedule gives her more time at home with a growing family, but when she does appear, Lopez remains a favorite of the fans.

Johnny Miller

United States

b. 1947

U.S. Open, 1973

British Open, 1976

For three years in the '70s, Johnny Miller ruled golf. The tall, blond San Franciscan's reign began at the 1973 U.S. Open at Oakmont where, six strokes off the lead starting the final round, he fired an unbelievable 63 and won. Weeks later, he finished second at the British Open. The next year, he was unstoppable, winning eight tournaments. He started 1975 with four victories, which included rounds in the low 60s. Miller soon tired of the tour life, though, and his game lost its sharpness. He won the 1976 British Open and managed the occasional success into the '80s, including his triumph at the 1987 AT&T Pebble Beach Pro-Am, where he exhibited his old form. He's now a respected television analyst.

The Morrises (father and son) of St. Andrews were among the first Scottish professionals. "Old Tom" caddied on the town's famous links, then apprenticed as a club- and ballmaker while honing his game. In 1851, he moved to Prestwick as custodian of the new club. The British Open began in 1860, and Old Tom was ready, winning it in 1861, '62, '64, and '67. In 1865, he returned to St. Andrews as greenskeeper. In 1868, "Young Tom" dethroned his father, winning the first of three straight Opens (he added another in 1872). Like his father, much of his fame came from exhibitions, firing scores in the 70s at a time when courses were rutted and wild. But Young Tom never had the chance to reach true greatness, dying at age twenty-five.

Old and Young Tom Morris

Scotland
1821–1908 and 1851–1875
British Open, 1861, 1862,
1864, 1867 (Morris, Sr.)
British Open, 1868, 1869,
1870, 1872 (Morris, Jr.)

"Lord Byron" has been an important player, innovator, and teacher. Coming out of the same Texas caddie ranks that produced Ben Hogan, Nelson is credited with the first "modern" golf swing, featuring a big, one-piece turn and power provided by the legs. After perfecting this motion in the early '30s, he won the 1937 Masters. His record is impressive—fifty-four wins, including two Masters (also 1942), the 1939 U.S. Open, and the PGA Championship in 1940 and '45. However, Nelson isn't remembered for any one victory as much as batches of them. In 1944 he won thirteen times, then returned in 1945 to win eleven straight events, eighteen in all; that year, he averaged 68.33 strokes per round. After five more wins in 1946, Nelson retired to his Texas ranch.

Byron Nelson

United States
b. 1912
U.S. Open, 1939
PGA Championship, 1940,
1945
Masters, 1937, 1942
Canadian Open, 1945

Jack Nicklaus

United States

b. 1940

U.S. Open, 1962, 1967, 1972, 1980

PGA Championship, 1963, 1971, 1973, 1975, 1980

Masters, 1963, 1965, 1966, 1972, 1975, 1986

U.S. Senior Open, 1991

British Open, 1966, 1970, 1978

Australian Open, 1968, 1971, 1975, 1976, 1978

Jack Nicklaus is the most influential and arguably the best golfer of all time. His record is astounding: nearly one hundred victories worldwide, including twenty major championships: two U.S. Amateurs, four U.S. Opens, three British Opens, five PGA Championships, and a record six Masters, capped by his heart-stopping victory in 1986 at age forty-six. He has earned more than $5 million in the United States, capturing eight money and eight scoring titles (with a career average under 71). His instruction books and videotapes are bestsellers as millions have tried to copy the famous upright swing, flying right elbow, and powerful leg drive. Today, in addition to playing on the Senior Tour, Nicklaus commands million-dollar fees as a course architect.

Greg Norman

Australia

b. 1955

British Open, 1986

Canadian Open, 1984

Australian Open, 1980, 1985, 1987

No one in golf has more charisma or talent than Greg Norman. The blond Australian learned the game at age seventeen with his mother's clubs and two Jack Nicklaus instruction books. He concentrated on hitting it hard and long, traits he still exhibits to the delight of crowds everywhere. He turned pro at age twenty-one, recording twenty-nine world victories before joining the U.S. Tour in 1984. Two years later, Norman started the final round of all four majors in the lead, but won only the British Open, losing to Nicklaus at Augusta, to Bob Tway at the PGA, and to his own temper at the U.S. Open. He still amasses money and fame, but has suffered nagging injuries and the barbs of the press about his inability to win big. But with his skills and smarts, don't count Norman out.

At age twenty, Francis Ouimet became America's first golf hero. The scene was the 1913 U.S. Open, played at The Country Club outside Boston, Massachusetts, and across the street from the Ouimet home. The former caddy found himself battling Britain's best, Harry Vardon and Ted Ray. Miraculously, Ouimet tied the two Englishmen, and in the next day's playoff beat Vardon by five strokes and Ray by six, making him only the second American to win his national championship. He went on to win the 1914 and '31 U.S. Amateurs. In 1951, after many years of service as a golf administrator, Ouimet was elected captain of the Royal and Ancient Golf Club of St. Andrews, Scotland, the first non-Briton so honored.

Francis Ouimet

United States

1893–1967

U.S. Open, 1913

U.S. Amateur, 1914, 1931

Arnold Palmer is the king with a common touch. He came out of western Pennsylvania with a slashing swing, a hitch of the pants, and the crowd-thrilling habit of firing at the flag. He won the 1954 U.S. Amateur, then turned pro, capturing sixty-one tour titles and setting numerous money records in nineteen years. But his legend was built on major titles, notably four Masters (1958, '60, '62, and '64). In 1960, he won his only U.S. Open —coming from seven strokes back in the final round— and made his first trip to the British Open, which he won in 1961 and '62. His successes benefited every part of the game, brought in fans ("Arnie's Army") and corporate sponsorship, and when his skills began to diminish, spurred the creation of the Senior Tour.

Arnold Palmer

United States

b. 1929

U.S. Open, 1960

Masters, 1958, 1960, 1962, 1964

British Open, 1961, 1962

Canadian Open, 1955

Australian Open, 1966

Gary Player

South Africa

b. 1935

U.S. Open, 1965

Masters, 1961, 1974, 1978

PGA Championship, 1962, 1972

U.S. Senior Open, 1987, 1988

British Open, 1959, 1968, 1974

Australian Open, 1958, 1962, 1963, 1965, 1969, 1970, 1974

No one works harder at golf than South African Gary Player. His strict regimens of diet, exercise, and practice have produced a golf game that is hardly pretty but always effective. Getting every bit of power possible from his small frame, Player has won more than 140 tournaments around the world, including 21 on the PGA Tour, nearly 20 (and counting) on the Senior Tour, 13 South African Opens, and 7 Australian Opens. He is one of only four men to win all four of the modern majors: The Masters (1961, '74, '78), U.S. Open (1965), PGA Championship (1962 and '72), and British Open (1959, '68, and '74). Throughout forty years as a professional, Player has proven that determination and hard work can overcome any obstacles.

Gene Sarazen

United States

b. 1902

U.S. Open, 1922, 1932

PGA Championship, 1922, 1923, 1933

Masters, 1935

British Open, 1932

Australian Open, 1936

A few years after taking up the game as therapy for pleurisy, this carpenter's son from New York won the 1922 U.S. Open and the 1922 and '23 PGA Championship. Sarazen then floundered for ten years before fighting back to capture the 1932 U.S. and British Opens, and 1933 PGA. The "Squire's" final major was The Masters of 1935, where he hit "the shot heard round the world," a 4-wood approach to Augusta's 15th that found the hole for a double eagle. It tied him with Craig Wood, whom he beat in the next day's playoff to become the first man to win all four modern majors. He remained competitive for a few more years, then brought charm and flair to his work as a television commentator.

Samuel Jackson Snead emerged from the Virginia woods in 1937 with a silky-smooth swing that produced 275-yard drives and deadly wedge shots with equal ease. He was still using much the same motion in 1979 when he became the first player to shoot his age in a regular tour event, firing 67 and 66 at age sixty-seven. Slammin' Sammy owns seven major titles — three Masters (1949, '52, '54), three PGA Championships (1942, '49, '51), and one British Open (1946) — and holds the record for PGA Tour wins, 84; include senior and international events and his victory total climbs to 135. Despite this record, Snead is also remembered for the tournament he came close to winning but never won, the U.S. Open. This omission is only a slight blot on a brilliant résumé.

Sam Snead

United States
b. 1912
PGA Championship, 1942, 1949, 1951
Masters, 1949, 1952, 1954
British Open, 1946
Canadian Open, 1938, 1940, 1941

Australian Peter Thomson's playing career was highlighted by five British Open wins (1954–56, '58, and '65), a feat surpassed only by Harry Vardon fifty years earlier and matched by Tom Watson twenty years later. Blessed with a simple swing and a complex mind, Thomson dominated Down Under, capturing nine New Zealand and three Australian Opens between 1950 and 1972. He also claimed numerous titles in Europe, but was less effective in the U.S., winning only once during his prime. But on the fledgling Senior Tour, he shone again, winning more than $1 million and eleven events — nine in 1985 alone. When not playing, Thomson designs courses, writes, leads the Australian PGA, and does charity work.

Peter Thomson

Australia
b. 1929
British Open, 1954, 1955, 1956, 1958, 1965
Australian Open, 1951, 1967, 1972

Walter J. Travis

Australia/United States
1862–1927
U.S. Amateur, 1900, 1901,
1903
British Amateur, 1904

Although he was known as the "Grand Old Man" because he didn't take up golf until age thirty-five, Walter Travis made up for lost time, winning the U.S. Amateur in 1900 and again in 1901 and '03. In 1904, he became the first non-Briton to win the British Amateur. Travis, who came to the United States from Australia as a young man, was a formidable presence thanks to an ever-present black cigar, a cantankerous manner, and a brilliant putting stroke. He needed the last because he was a small man, regularly outhit by opponents. While remaining competitive into his fifties, Travis gained notoriety as founder and editor of *The American Golfer*, an early influential magazine, and as a course architect.

Lee Trevino

United States
b. 1939
U.S. Open, 1968, 1971
PGA Championship, 1974,
1984
U.S. Senior Open, 1990
British Open, 1971, 1972
Canadian Open, 1971, 1977,
1979

There are two Lee Trevinos. The public loves the wise-cracking "Merry Mex," who pulled himself up from a dirt-poor Texas childhood. Then there is the serious Trevino, who marshals his concentration and dissects the golf course with a controlled fade and precise shot-making. He struggled for seven years as a pro before finishing fifth at the 1967 U.S. Open. The next year he was Open champion. Trevino's greatest year was 1971, when he won a second U.S. Open, then the Canadian and British Opens, all within three weeks. The British Open fell again in 1972, the PGA Championship in 1974 and '84. Add many international titles and domination of the Senior Tour in his rookie year, 1990. There is no golfer more competitive, and few who have come so far.

One of the greatest and most influential golfers in history, Harry Vardon came from Jersey, in the Channel Islands, and won the British Open a record six times (1896, '98, '99, 1903, '11, '14). His upright, rhythmic swing and overlapping grip became the ideals. He was a long hitter for his average size, and deadly accurate. It was said that if he played the same course twice in a day, he'd hit the afternoon's shots out of the morning's divots. (The PGA Tour award for low scoring average is appropriately called the Vardon Trophy.) In 1900, while touring the United States promoting a golf ball, Vardon won the U.S. Open; he finished runner-up in 1913 and '20 (at age fifty). From 1903 until his death, he was a club pro, wrote on golf, and designed courses.

Harry Vardon

Britain

1870–1937

U.S. Open, 1900

British Open, 1896, 1898, 1899, 1903, 1911, 1914

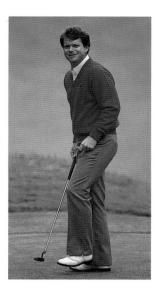

For the first few years of his pro career, Tom Watson was labeled a "choker." He was good enough to contend, but found ways to lose. Even taking the 1975 British Open didn't silence the skeptics. That happened in 1977 when Watson held off Jack Nicklaus to win both the Masters and British Open. Starting then, he dominated for eight years, winning nearly thirty tour titles, plus money and scoring awards. His record in the majors is one of the best — five British Opens (1975, '77, '80, '82–3), two Masters (1977 and '81), and, most memorable, the 1982 U.S. Open, where he topped Nicklaus with a chip-in from deep rough at Pebble Beach's 17th hole. Despite losing his putting skills in the late '80s, he is still an intense competitor and crowd favorite.

Tom Watson

United States

b. 1949

U.S. Open, 1982

Masters, 1977, 1981

British Open, 1975, 1977, 1980, 1982, 1983

Australian Open, 1984

Mickey Wright

United States

b. 1935

U.S. Women's Open, 1958, 1959, 1961, 1964

LPGA Championship, 1958, 1960, 1961, 1963

San Diego–born Mickey Wright came along when the LPGA Tour was new and helped it gain respect. She turned pro after a fine amateur career, and, by 1958, was the leading female player. That year she won the LPGA Championship and U.S. Open to become the first woman to win two majors in one season. In all, she prevailed in four Opens and four LPGAs, plus two Titleholders Championships and three Women's Western Opens (both now-defunct majors). On tour, she amassed eighty-two victories, was victorious at least once a year for fourteen years (1956–69), and took five consecutive scoring titles (1960–64). As an officer and spokesperson of the LPGA, Wright was instrumental in its growth, before retiring to Florida in the late '70s.

Babe Zaharias

United States

1914–1956

U.S. Women's Open, 1948, 1950, 1954

The day after earning two gold medals for track in the 1932 Olympics, Mildred Didrikson Zaharias played a round of golf, belting the ball farther than most men and breaking 100; soon she was touring the United States, giving long-ball exhibitions. During the Second World War, after Tommy Armour taught her shot-making and a short game to complement her power, she claimed her first important titles, three straight Women's Western Opens. In 1947, she became the first American to win the British Ladies' Championship. Zaharias went on to win thirty-one events between 1948 and 1955, including three U.S. Opens (1948, '50, '54), the last won after she underwent surgery for the cancer that claimed her, too young and too soon, in 1956.

If you've seen one tennis court, you've seen them all. Is there any point comparing a bowling alley in Montreal with one in Miami? And what's the difference between a soccer field in Britain and one in Burma or Bolivia? While each no doubt reflects some local color, these fields of play are uniform because their sports dictate that the court or pitch or lane be exactly so wide and so long the world over.

That is, thankfully, not the case in golf. Every hole on every course is unique. How a bulldozer operator or an architect chooses to mold the land is what makes each hole a world unto itself. And because each hole is distinctive, it is inevitable that some are regarded as better than others, which, in turn, leads to lists like this one.

Here, then, are one man's picks of eighteen great holes. They are not necessarily the hardest, certainly not the longest, definitely not the trickiest. Yet each one brings something special to the game — a touch of beauty, a nuance of design, or the capacity to bring out the best in those who play it.

Obviously there are hundreds of holes that could have been chosen, and my apologies if your favorites have been overlooked. But give these a look and see if we agree on what makes a great hole ''great.''

Eighteen Great Holes

Yale Golf Club, 9th hole.

Cypress Point Club, 16th hole.

16th Hole — Cypress Point Club, Pebble Beach, California, USA

Par 3

233 yards

It has been called the "most beautiful golf hole in the world." For years, it was also the most difficult hole on the PGA Tour, averaging more than half a stroke over par. Although the very private Cypress Point no longer hosts the AT&T Pebble Beach Pro-Am, its spectacular par-three continues to captivate as golfers everywhere wonder if they could tame it.

Good luck to them. The hole is a visual feast, playing over an inlet of the Pacific Ocean where waves crash on the gray rocks below. At 233 yards, it almost always requires a driver because the prevailing wind is smack into the golfer's face. The roar of the surf drowns out all other noise except the chattering of teeth as golfers worry about finding the ocean, one of the greenside traps, or the wiry ice-plant rough. There is a safe area short of the green; however, few people aim for it: if they're there, they've probably hit a bad, albeit lucky, shot. Tournament scores have soared as high as 19, but the hole has yielded a few aces as well. Those are the extremes proving that par is an enviable achievement.

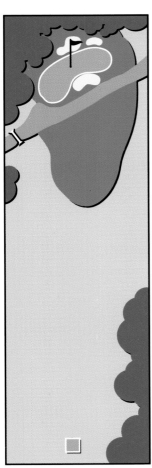

Par 3

155 yards

12th Hole—Augusta National Golf Club, Augusta, Georgia, USA

Jack Nicklaus has called this "the greatest tournament hole in the world," strong praise for a straightaway par-three of 155 yards, the shortest hole on the course. During The Masters, however, it regularly ranks as the hardest hole. What makes it so tough? Sand, water, and wind, to say nothing of mental pressure. There isn't a player in the field who doesn't know that Tom Weiskopf took a 13 here in 1980, and in 1991 Nicklaus carded a 7.

The keys to success at the 12th are yardage and club selection to combat the swirling wind and the very narrow target presented by the green, which runs perpendicular to the tee shot. The ball that comes up short will splash into either Rae's Creek or the bunker tucked, front and center, into the green. Hitting long isn't much better. Two bunkers behind the green slope up to the back; find either of them and it takes a delicate shot to stay on the green—and out of the water. Hit way long and there's a wall of thick shrubs to contend with. What's that saying about good things coming in small packages?

51

Par 3

250 yards

9th Hole—Yale Golf Club, New Haven, Connecticut, USA

The official yardage guide calls this long par-three "most unusual," and so it is. From the back tees to the end of the green, the hole is 250 yards long, with more than half that carry over a pond. The green is long—70 yards stem to stern—so a seemingly easy target. But cutting across it is an 8-foot-deep depression that has the effect of creating two greens, front and back, with a roller-coaster dip separating them. Whichever tier holds the flag, you'd better be there.

Yale was the creation of Charles Blair Macdonald, who was instrumental in exposing America to golf before the turn of the century. He learned the game from Old Tom Morris while a student in St. Andrews, Scotland. In time, he designed more than a dozen courses, including the first eighteen-hole layout in the United States (the Chicago Golf Club). He also was a leading player of his day, winning the first U.S. Amateur, in 1895. But to do so, he twice had to have earlier attempts at a national championship, both of which he lost, expunged from the record books. Macdonald was a strange but powerful fellow, and the 9th at Yale reflects those qualities.

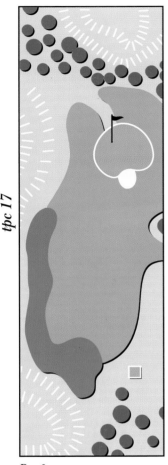

Par 3

132 yards

17th Hole — Tournament Players Club at Sawgrass, Ponte Vedra, Florida, USA

The 17th at Sawgrass may not be the most famous hole in golf, but it's among the most infamous. Its green, only slightly larger than a lily pad, is the ultimate in target golf, daring players to go after it. Pros and amateurs call it many things, most unprintable. It is best known simply as the ''island hole,'' a 132-yard par-three that has soured more stomachs than bad Mexican food.

The hole is easy to describe: tee, 100 yards of water, and a circular green that architect Pete Dye made less than 70 feet wide at any point. The surface is two-tiered and slightly crowned. Unless a ball sits down quickly, it can hit safe but still roll, bounce, or spin into the drink. There is no bail-out except a tiny pot bunker at the front of the green, and no strategy except getting the ball to stay put. Approximately 50,000 golf balls are fished out of the water each year. Some are left there by PGA Tour pros during the Players Championship, but most come off the clubs of the amateurs who keep tee times at Sawgrass booked all year long.

53

Par 4

446 yards

13th Hole — Pine Valley Golf Club, Pine Valley, New Jersey, USA

In 1912, Philadelphia hotelier George Crump gazed out the window as his train rumbled across southern New Jersey and thought the scrubby, sandy landscape was the perfect setting for a golf course of uncommon difficulty. Pine Valley is the culmination of Crump's dream, 184 acres of bunker dotted with specks of fairway and even smaller greens. It is ''penal'' architecture carried to extremes, golf as might be designed by the Marquis de Sade.

Everything great and gruesome about Pine Valley awaits the player at the 13th, a long (446-yard) par-four. The tee shot must fly straight and at least 175 yards to an island of grass amid a sea of sand. If the drive is properly placed, the green comes into view, tucked to the left behind pine trees. It beckons enticingly, but demands a perfect long-iron or fairway-wood shot over another Saharan expanse. Closer and safer, a patch of fairway fronts the green. So, that's the challenge: go for it in two or play for a pitch and a putt. All the holes pose similar dilemmas, explaining why golfers are drawn to Pine Valley: it frightens, exhilarates, and tells them what they're made of.

Par 4

305 yards

10th Hole (West Course) — Royal Melbourne Golf Club, Melbourne, Victoria, Australia

The two courses at Royal Melbourne were designed in 1926 by Alex Russell, an Australian Open champion, and Alister Mackenzie, an English-born doctor who gave up medicine for golf architecture and became one of the craft's finest practitioners, as well as one of the first to work internationally. Mackenzie's legacy includes the Eden Course at St. Andrews, California's Cypress Point, and layouts from Argentina to Ireland. Mackenzie also collaborated with Bobby Jones on Augusta National, the course that best exemplifies the good doctor's prescription for strategic design.

The 10th on Royal Melbourne's West Course (it becomes number 8 on the Composite Course used to host major events) is another example of Mackenzie's brilliance. A 305-yard dogleg left, the green can be driven, but that risks catching the huge bunker tucked in the crook. The conservative play is a straight drive, which should leave a short pitch to the tiny green. But the tee shot must fly just far enough to crest a broad valley dissecting the fairway; coming up short leaves a blind shot, and too long means toying with two greenside bunkers on the approach. That combination of choice and challenge showcases Mackenzie in top form.

Pine Valley Golf Club, 13th hole.

Tournament Players Club at Sawgrass, 17th hole.

Augusta National Golf Club, 12th hole.

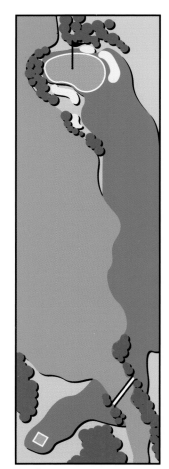

Par 4

433 yards

5th Hole — Mid Ocean Club, Tucker's Town, Bermuda

Only 20 square miles but with ten courses, Bermuda could boast the greatest density of golf in the world. By far the best is at the Mid Ocean Club, another C.B. Macdonald design (see Yale GC), which means another formidable challenge from the old school. Macdonald's original dates to 1924; a reworking by Robert Trent Jones in the 1950s kept intact the course's mix of brutality and fairness.

The 433-yard, par-four 5th is world-famous. Called "Cape," it copies an idea Macdonald put into practice at the National Golf Links on New York's Long Island — the heroic carry over water to an angled fairway. Just how heroic depends on the golfer's nerve. From the elevated tee, it's hard to judge the distance over Mangrove Lake; 200 yards is a good estimate, with a bailout area to the right for the faint of heart. Babe Ruth, never one to play safe, reportedly left a dozen balls in the lake, trying to drive the green. Finding the fairway doesn't end the difficulties: the hole continues arcing along the water's edge, and two long bunkers embrace the green. Bermuda tourism officials are wise not to showcase this hole in their brochures. It would spoil their island's reputation for tranquility.

15th Hole — Oakmont Country Club, Oakmont, Pennsylvania, USA

Par 4

453 yards

Laid out in 1903 by steel magnate Henry Fownes and his son William, Oakmont has hosted five U.S. Opens and three PGA Championships, and been a stern test each time, rarely yielding scores under par. The notable exception was Johnny Miller's final-round 63 in the 1973 Open, quite simply one of the greatest rounds ever played. Oakmont's difficulty lies in its ultra-fast greens and acres of sand. The Fowneses positioned 220 bunkers; about 190 exist today, some in odd shapes and sizes, all capable of wreaking havoc.

Number 15 is a par-four playing to 450-plus yards from the back tees, with fairway bunkers that collect many "good" drives. But it is the 95-yard-long, 15-yard-wide bunker, which starts 30 yards ahead of, then runs along the right side of the green, that is the killer. There are also greenside bunkers left that limit the possibilities for bailing out. In the 1953 U.S. Open, Ben Hogan had to chip out sideways from the right fairway bunker and hit a long-iron approach. He put it to 20 feet, holed the putt, and went on to top Sam Snead by six strokes.

18th Hole — Doral Country Club (Blue Course), Miami, Florida, USA

Par 4

425 yards

There are ninety-eight holes at the Doral Resort and Country Club, and then there is the "Blue Monster." This 425-yard par-four is notorious for dashing the dreams of tour pros preparing their victory speeches. Since 1962, when the course opened and the first Doral Open was held, the Monster has regularly ranked among the hardest holes on the tour.

Dick Wilson designed the snake-like 18th to slither right to left along one of the course's eight manmade lakes. Although a good tee shot and approach don't have to cross the lake, the temptation to be bold is strong. Because it's difficult to judge distance over water, many shots that begin looking good finish wet. The right side offers safety, but lengthens the hole and brings two greenside bunkers into play; a bladed shot from either one probably will find the lake.

While managing the 18th is its own reward, successful amateurs are given a pin that reads: "I parred the Blue Monster." It is the golfer's badge of honor.

Par 4
458 yards

18th Hole — Harbour Town Golf Links, Hilton Head Island, South Carolina, USA

Jack Nicklaus, the greatest golfer of all time, and Pete Dye, the leading iconoclast of golf architecture, collaborated on a course design only once. The result is as strong as anything either has laid out alone. Harbour Town, opened in 1969 and open to the public, is a testing track that winds through mossy stands of pine, oak, and magnolia, and embraces marshes, ponds, and other soggy bogs. Not a long course, it demands precision rather than power.

The final hole is the perfect climax. The tee, landing area, and tiny green of this 458-yard par-four jut into a salt marsh that separates the fairway from Calibogue Sound (pronounced ''Calla-bogey,'' like double bogey). The drive must fly straight at least 200 yards toward the famous red and white Harbour Town lighthouse: go left and it's briny; go right and it's pinball among palm trees and condos. The daring approach flirts with the marsh and sand, or can be played cautiously toward the right. But even the careful way can become no way if the wind is up off the Sound. Like ships heading toward a beacon, some golfers find this hole a safe haven, while others crash just short of home.

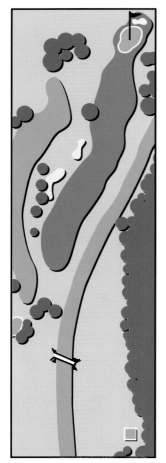

Par 4

420 yards

14th Hole — Glen Abbey Golf Club, Oakville, Ontario, Canada

There is no shortage of irony in the fact that Glen Abbey Golf Club, which has hosted the Canadian Open every year but one since 1977, was designed by Jack Nicklaus: although Nicklaus has won twenty major tournaments and many other prestigious events, he has never captured the Canadian. He's come close, with a record seven second-place finishes, but has always found a way to come up short.

Nothing else at Glen Abbey comes up short. The course is long and tough, the landscape majestic, and the list of champions strong, including Lee Trevino, Greg Norman, and Curtis Strange (twice). Also not short is 16 Mile Creek, which meanders through the back nine and plays a prominent role at the 420-yard, par-four 14th. The tee shot has to carry the creek, which slices across the hole at an angle, forcing golfers to cut off as much as they dare. Play too safe and the fairway bunkers and pond across the fairway suddenly loom large. The mid- to long-iron approach is to a slightly elevated green bisected by a tricky hollow. Triple- and quadruple-breakers are the rule, making short work of any hope for par.

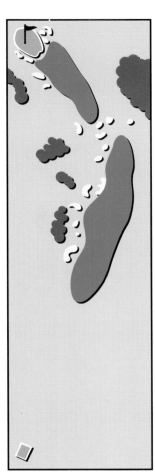

Par 4

413 yards

17th Hole—Royal Lytham & St. Annes Golf Club, Lancashire, England

If the three English courses on the British Open rota—St. George's, Birkdale, and Lytham—are not as well known as their Scottish cousins, it is not for want of history. Lytham could be the most memorable, having been the site of Bobby Jones's first Open, in 1926. It is also where Englishman Tony Jacklin won in 1969, ending an eighteen-year string of foreign champions. Other Lytham Opens have been won by Bobby Locke, Peter Thomson, Gary Player, and Seve Ballesteros, but it is Jones's victory, secured at the 17th, that stands out.

Today, as in 1926, the hole is a narrow dogleg-left with bunkers splattered down the left side. The obvious smart shot is to the right, but Jones, battling Walter Hagen and another American, Al Watrous, in the final round, found one of the bunkers to the left, about 175 yards from the hole. Unable to see the green but all too aware of the sandhills, rough, and other trouble on his line, Jones hit a mashie (4-iron), picking the ball cleanly and dropping it on the green. Watrous, who'd taken the safe route to the green, three-putted after Jones's magnificent display. A plaque on the spot honors Jones, and reminds today's golfer that, if he's nearby, he's in the wrong place.

Glen Abbey Golf Club, 14th hole.

Royal Lytham and St. Annes Golf Club, 17th hole.

65

Harbour Town Golf Links, 18th hole.

Par 4

448 yards

18th Hole — Muirfield, East Lothian, Scotland

The course is known as Muirfield, but it is formally The Honourable Company of Edinburgh Golfers, the oldest golf club in the world, dating to 1744. The present site has been the club's home since 1891, and is considered the fairest of the British Open tests — a classic blend of flat land, heavy rough, persistent wind, and menacing bunkers. Rich in tradition, Muirfield has hosted fourteen Opens (including 1992).

It is said that to conquer Muirfield, one must drive well. The straightaway, 448-yard, par-four final hole exemplifies that. The tee is slightly elevated, so the five fairway bunkers — three in the middle of the hole, two within 50 yards of the green — are easily seen. But seeing is not the same as avoiding. The bunkers pinch the landing area and define the route to the smallish green, which is itself hemmed in by sand. The green sits just a few yards from the Muirfield clubhouse, which contains paintings, medals, old clubs and balls, and other memorabilia that provide a link to golf's past. As if this hole weren't difficult enough, proximity to the game's roots makes it all the more daunting.

17th Hole — Old Course at St. Andrews, St. Andrews, Scotland

Par 4

461 yards

For more than four hundred years, golf has been played over the Old Course. It's open to the public, meaning visiting players can test themselves against the game's history, much of which was made during the twenty-four British Opens contested at St. Andrews since 1873. The Open returns to the Old Course in 1995. It's certain to be special, and likely that the 17th hole will figure in the outcome.

Until recently the drive had to carry railway sheds; today, it's a hotel outbuilding that makes the tee shot almost blind. Starting at about the landing area, the fairway bends gently right. But the green, which is slightly elevated, angles back to the left, limiting the chance of success with a long run-up. The approach is key: to the right of the green is the macadam road that gives the "Road Hole" its name; tucked into the green's left side is the nefarious Road Bunker, deep and dastardly; laying up for a short pitch makes sense, but the front half of the green funnels toward the bunker. As long as golf is played, this hole will be one of the great ones, and players will wonder how, if at all, they can conquer it.

18th Hole—Pebble Beach Golf Links, Pebble Beach, California, USA

Par 5
548 yards

Sometimes an architect's genius is knowing when *not* to make his mark. Such was the case at Pebble Beach, which is the work of Jack Neville, a three-time California amateur champion who had no design experience when he was asked to build a course on the rocky bluffs above the Pacific Ocean in 1915. Neville took his cue from nature. He moved very little dirt, acknowledging that nothing he could create would be more spectacular than what he started with. He succeeded admirably — and never worked on another course.

The final hole may be the finest finish of them all, a 548-yard par-five that curves right to left along the ocean. The tee shot has to bite off some of the sea to finish right-center, but not too far right or it flirts with trees. The second shot also should stay right, but more trees line that side. Most players will still face a wedge to a green boxed in by bunkers. If all that weren't enough, wind usually whips in off the water. And don't forget the ocean, crashing and roaring just a few feet away, singing a siren song to any mishit shot — and many a player's best intentions.

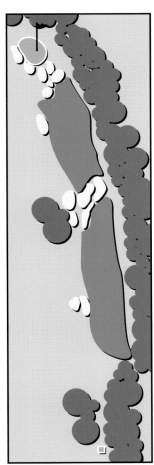

Par 5

630 yards

17th Hole (Lower Course) — Baltusrol Golf Club, Springfield, New Jersey, USA

Baltusrol is a club of grand dimensions, from its stately gabled clubhouse to its two courses, both of which have hosted U.S. Opens (men's and women's). The more famous of the two, the Lower, was laid out by A.W. Tillinghast in the 1920s, then remodeled by Robert Trent Jones in the 1950s. It is a broad-shouldered design, 7,000-plus yards from the back tees. But par is 70, which means there are only two par-fives. Strangely, they come back-to-back; uniquely, they are the final two holes.

Number 17 is the killer, at 630 yards. The premium is on length; however, most golfers can't simply bang away because the second shot flirts with the maze of bunkers, called the ''Sahara Desert,'' that divides the fairway about 400 yards out. Laying up is often the smart play, but that still leaves more than 200 yards to the green, which is guarded by another phalanx of traps. So forget about hitting this hole in two and worry about hitting it in *four*. And then there is still the 18th to play, 542 yards of it. That's two-thirds of a mile over the last two holes.

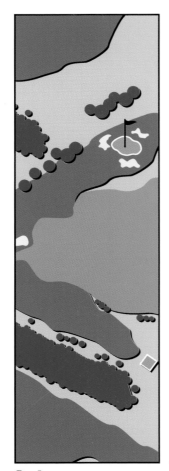

Par 5

575 yards

13th Hole — Dunes Golf and Beach Club, Myrtle Beach, South Carolina, USA

After the Second World War, Robert Trent Jones emerged as the world's preeminent course architect, a position he held for thirty-plus years. During that time he designed or remodeled more than five hundred courses. His creations run to the big and bold, featuring long tee boxes; vast, undulating greens; abundant water and sand; and yardage galore. Mixing distance and the possibility of disaster made Jones's courses popular venues for major tournaments. Among his better-known creations are the Lower Course at Baltusrol, Firestone (South), Hazeltine National, and Oakland Hills — all U.S. Open and/or PGA Championship sites.

Jones also laid out many public-access courses. One of the best is The Dunes, which opened in 1947 and helped launch Myrtle Beach, where there are now nearly a hundred clubs catering to vacationing golfers. The Dunes is long (7,000 yards) and tough, nowhere more so than at the 575-yard, par-five 13th, which doglegs almost back on itself around Singleton Lake. The bend is greater than a right angle, and invites a prototypical Jones heroic shot — a fairway wood into a stiff breeze and across the water. Length alone isn't enough, though, since three bunkers surround the green. Temptation and trouble should be Jones's middle names.

13th Hole — Augusta National Golf Club, Augusta, Georgia, USA

It is the rare golf course that places two holes in this, or any, ranking of great holes. But Augusta National is rare indeed, and this list would be incomplete without both the par-three 12th and this par-five, a hole that Curtis Strange, Greg Norman, and many others call the greatest in golf.

It's interesting to note that this hole is 20 yards shorter than Augusta's 10th hole, a par-four. The difference is terrain and shape. Where the 10th runs straight and drops more than 100 feet downhill, the 13th is flat and doglegs left past a thick stand of trees and along Rae's Creek. Although the perfect tee shot is a draw, shortening the hole, it's not unusual to see drives pushed right — leaving an approach from more trees and off a downhill, sidehill lie — or hooked into the water. The second shot is crucial: lay up short of the creek, which meanders back into play, or go for a green backed by bunkers? In the 1985 Masters, Strange was in command in the final round until he tried the heroic route. He dunked his 4-wood shot into the water, drowning both his ball and his hopes for victory.

Par 5

485 yards

Pebble Beach Golf Links,
18th hole.

Augusta National Golf
Club, 13th hole.

Muirfield, 18th hole.

Baltusrol Golf Club, 17th hole (lower course).

Great Courses Anyone Can —and Should— Play

Even if you don't belong to a country club, and even if you don't have a pro-quality golf game, you still can play some of the greatest and most famous courses in the world. Many top tracks are open to the public, because they are either daily-fee (green fees can be expensive, up to $150 and more for a single round) or part of a resort (resort-associated courses are indicated by *; some require you to be a guest at the resort to arrange a tee time).

Ballybunion Golf Club (Old), Ballybunion, Co. Kerry, Ireland
Banff Springs Golf Club, Banff, Alberta, Canada*
Bethpage State Park (Black), Farmingdale, New York, USA
Cape Breton Highlands Links, Cape Breton Highlands National Park, Nova Scotia, Canada*
Casa de Campo (Teeth of the Dog), La Romana, Dominican Republic*
Cascades (Upper), The Homestead, Hot Springs, Virginia, USA*
Concord (Championship), Kiamesha Lake, New York, USA*
Dorado Beach Hotel Club (East), Dorado, Puerto Rico*
Doral Resort and Country Club (Blue), Miami, Florida, USA*
Dunes Golf and Beach Club, Myrtle Beach, South Carolina, USA
Gleneagles (Kings), Auchterarder, Scotland*
Harbour Town Golf Links, Hilton Head Island, South Carolina, USA*
Jasper Park Lodge Golf Club, Jasper, Alberta, Canada*

Kauai Lagoons Golf and Racquet Club (Kiele), Lihue, Kauai, Hawaii, USA*

La Costa Resort and Spa, Carlsbad, California, USA*

Pasatiempo Golf Club, Santa Cruz, California, USA

Pebble Beach Golf Links, Pebble Beach, California, USA*

PGA West (Stadium), La Quinta, California, USA*

Pinehurst Country Club (No. 2), Pinehurst, North Carolina, USA*

Port Royal Golf Course, Southampton, Bermuda

Spyglass Hill Golf Course, Pebble Beach, California, USA

St. Andrews (Old Course), St. Andrews, Scotland

TPC at Sawgrass, Ponte Vedra, Florida, USA*

Turnberry Golf Club (Ailsa), Turnberry, Scotland*

Waterville Golf Links, Co. Kerry, Ireland*

Wild Dunes (Links), Isle of Palms, South Carolina, USA*

Fairways and Green

Once upon a time, golf was not about money. Or at least that's what players from the "good old days" like to tell us. They say they played for the trophy, for first place, to be the best, and that the check didn't matter. When the winner of a Tour event collected only $600 (and by tenth place there was barely enough to pay for gas), playing for glory made sense.

That's not the way things are today.

In 1990, Greg Norman led the PGA Tour in official earnings, with $1,165,477. A pretty good year. But Norman didn't make as much as Senior Tour rookie Lee Trevino, who banked $1,190,518 — an incredible amount when you realize that there was no Senior Tour until 1980.

Trevino has been around long enough to remember when Jack Nicklaus could top the Tour money makers in 1967 with under $200,000 — which is less than Steve Elkington took home for winning the 1990 Kmart Greater Greensboro Open. Professional golf has come a long way.

The women, too, are playing for real money now. Beth Daniel amassed $863,578 in 1990, ten times as much as the season's leading money winner, JoAnne Carner, made in 1974.

Is there too much money? Some critics say the huge purses have crushed golfers' competitive spirit. Maybe winning becomes secondary when the 75th man on the PGA Tour money list can expect to earn upward of $200,000. From that he has to pay travel expenses, caddies, entry fees, even laundry bills, and, of course, taxes. But it's still a pretty good living. Some would say it beats working.

Past Leading PGA Tour Money-Winners

Year	Winner	Amount	Year	Winner	Amount	Year	Winner	Amount	Year	Winner	Amount
1934	Paul Runyan	$6,767	1949	Sam Snead	31,593	1966	Billy Casper	121,944	1983	Hal Sutton	426,688
1935	Johnny Revolta	9,543	1950	Sam Snead	35,758	1967	Jack Nicklaus	188,998	1984	Tom Watson	476,260
1936	Horton Smith	7,682	1951	Lloyd Mangrum	26,088	*1968	Billy Casper	205,168	1985	Curtis Strange	542,321
1937	Harry Cooper	14,138	1952	Julius Boros	37,032	1969	Frank Beard	164,707	1986	Greg Norman	653,296
1938	Sam Snead	19,534	1953	Lew Worsham	34,002	1970	Lee Trevino	157,037	1987	Curtis Strange	925,941
1939	Henry Picard	10,303	1954	Bob Toski	65,819	1971	Jack Nicklaus	244,490	1988	Curtis Strange	1,147,644
1940	Ben Hogan	10,655	1955	Julius Boros	63,121	1972	Jack Nicklaus	320,542	1989	Tom Kite	1,395,278
1941	Ben Hogan	18,358	1956	Ted Kroll	72,835	1973	Jack Nicklaus	308,362	1990	Greg Norman	1,165,477
1942	Ben Hogan	13,143	1957	Dick Mayer	65,835	1974	Johnny Miller	353,021	1991	Corey Pavin	979,430
1943	No statistics compiled		1958	Arnold Palmer	42,607	#1975	Jack Nicklaus	298,149			
1944	Byron Nelson		1959	Art Wall	53,167	1976	Jack Nicklaus	266,438			
	(War Bonds)	37,967	1960	Arnold Palmer	75,262	1977	Tom Watson	310,653			
1945	Byron Nelson		1961	Gary Player	64,540	1978	Tom Watson	362,428			
	(War Bonds)	63,335	1962	Arnold Palmer	81,448	1979	Tom Watson	462,636		*Total money listed, beginning in	
1946	Ben Hogan	42,556	1963	Arnold Palmer	128,230	1980	Tom Watson	530,808		1968 and through to 1974	
1947	Jimmy Demaret	27,936	1964	Jack Nicklaus	113,284	1981	Tom Kite	375,698		#Official money listed, beginning	
1948	Ben Hogan	32,112	1965	Jack Nicklaus	140,752	1982	Craig Stadler	446,462		in 1975	

Past Leading Senior Tour Money-Winners

Year	Winner	Amount	Year	Winner	Amount	Year	Winner	Amount	Year	Winner	Amount
1980	Don January	$44,100	1983	Don January	237,571	1986	Bruce Crampton	454,299	1989	Bob Charles	725,887
1981	Miller Barber	83,136	1984	Don January	328,597	1987	Chi Chi Rodriguez	509,145	1990	Lee Trevino	1,190,518
1982	Miller Barber	106,890	1985	Peter Thomson	386,724	1988	Bob Charles	533,929	1991	Mike Hill	1,065,657

Past Leading LPGA Tour Money-Winners

Year	Winner	Amount	Year	Winner	Amount	Year	Winner	Amount	Year	Winner	Amount
1950	Babe Zaharias	$14,800	1961	Mickey Wright	22,236	1972	Kathy Whitworth	65,063	1983	JoAnne Carner	291,404
1951	Babe Zaharias	15,087	1962	Mickey Wright	21,641	1973	Kathy Whitworth	82,864	1984	Betsy King	266,771
1952	Betsy Rawls	14,505	1963	Mickey Wright	31,269	1974	JoAnne Carner	87,094	1985	Nancy Lopez	416,472
1953	Louise Suggs	19,816	1964	Mickey Wright	29,800	1975	Sandra Palmer	76,374	1986	Pat Bradley	492,021
1954	Patty Berg	16,011	1965	Kathy Whitworth	28,658	1976	Judy Rankin	150,734	1987	Ayako Okamoto	466,034
1955	Patty Berg	16,492	1966	Kathy Whitworth	33,517	1977	Judy Rankin	122,890	1988	Sherri Turner	350,851
1956	Marlene Hagge	20,235	1967	Kathy Whitworth	32,937	1978	Nancy Lopez	189,814	1989	Betsy King	654,132
1957	Patty Berg	16,272	1968	Kathy Whitworth	48,379	1979	Nancy Lopez	197,489	1990	Beth Daniel	863,578
1958	Beverly Hanson	12,639	1969	Carol Mann	49,152	1980	Beth Daniel	231,000	1991	Pat Bradley	763,118
1959	Betsy Rawls	26,774	1970	Kathy Whitworth	30,235	1981	Beth Daniel	206,998			
1960	Louise Suggs	16,892	1971	Kathy Whitworth	41,181	1982	JoAnne Carner	310,400			

Tour Winners

The Masters Tournament

Augusta National Golf Club
Augusta, Georgia

Year	Winner	Score
1934	Horton Smith	284
1935	*Gene Sarazen	282
1936	Horton Smith	285
1937	Byron Nelson	283
1938	Henry Picard	285
1939	Ralph Guldahl	279
1940	Jimmy Demaret	280
1941	Craig Wood	280
1942	*Byron Nelson	280
1943–45	*No tournament— Second World War*	
1946	Herman Keiser	282
1947	Jimmy Demaret	281
1948	Claude Harmon	279
1949	Sam Snead	282
1950	Jimmy Demaret	283
1951	Ben Hogan	280
1952	Sam Snead	286
1953	Ben Hogan	274
1954	*Sam Snead	289
1955	Cary Middlecoff	279
1956	Jack Burke, Jr.	289
1957	Doug Ford	282
1958	Arnold Palmer	284
1959	Art Wall, Jr.	284
1960	Arnold Palmer	282
1961	Gary Player	280
1962	*Arnold Palmer	280
1963	Jack Nicklaus	286
1964	Arnold Palmer	276
1965	Jack Nicklaus	271
1966	*Jack Nicklaus	288
1967	Gay Brewer, Jr.	280
1968	Bob Goalby	277
1969	George Archer	281
1970	*Billy Casper	279
1971	Charles Coody	279
1972	Jack Nicklaus	286
1973	Tommy Aaron	283
1974	Gary Player	278
1975	Jack Nicklaus	276
1976	Ray Floyd	271
1977	Tom Watson	276
1978	Gary Player	277
1979	*Fuzzy Zoeller	280
1980	Seve Ballesteros	275
1981	Tom Watson	280
1982	*Craig Stadler	284
1983	Seve Ballesteros	280
1984	Ben Crenshaw	277
1985	Bernhard Langer	282
1986	Jack Nicklaus	279
1987	*Larry Mize	285
1988	Sandy Lyle	281
1989	*Nick Faldo	283
1990	*Nick Faldo	278
1991	Ian Woosnam	277

*Winner in playoff.

United States Open Championship

Year	Winner	Score	Location
1895	Horace Rawlins	173 (36 holes)	Newport GC, Newport, RI
1896	James Foulis	152 (36 holes)	Shinnecock Hills GC, Shinnecock Hills, NY
1897	Joe Lloyd	162 (36 holes)	Chicago GC, Wheaton, IL
1898	Fred Herd	328 (72 holes)	Myopia Hunt Club, Hamilton, MA
1899	Willie Smith	315	Baltimore CC, Baltimore, MD
1900	Harry Vardon	313	Chicago GC, Wheaton, IL
1901	*Willie Anderson	331	Myopia Hunt Club, Hamilton, MA
1902	Laurie Auchterlonie	307	Garden City GC, Garden City, NY
1903	*Willie Anderson	307	Baltusrol GC, Short Hills, NJ
1904	Willie Anderson	303	Glen View Club, Golf IL
1905	Willie Anderson	314	Myopia Hunt Club, Hamilton, MA
1906	Alex Smith	295	Onwentsia Club, Lake Forest, IL
1907	Alex Ross	302	Philadelphia Cricket Club, Chestnut Hill, PA
1908	*Fred McLeod	322	Myopia Hunt Club, Hamilton, MA
1909	George Sargent	290	Englewood GC, Englewood, NJ
1910	*Alex Smith	298	Philadelphia Cricket Club, Chestnut Hill, PA
1911	*John McDermott	307	Chicago GC, Wheaton, IL
1912	John McDermott	294	CC of Buffalo, Buffalo, NY
1913	*Francis Ouimet	304	The Country Club, Brookline, MA
1914	Walter Hagen	290	Midlothian CC, Blue Island, IL
1915	Jerome Travers	297	Baltusrol GC, Short Hills, NJ
1916	Charles Evans, Jr.	286	Minikahda Club, Minneapolis, MN
1917–18	No championships played — First World War		
1919	*Walter Hagen	301	Brae Burn CC, West Newton, MA
1920	Edward Ray	295	Inverness CC, Toledo, OH
1921	James M. Barnes	289	Columbia CC, Chevy Chase, MD
1922	Gene Sarazen	288	Skokie CC, Glencoe, IL
1923	*R. T. Jones, Jr.	296	Inwood CC, Inwood, LI, NY
1924	Cyril Walker	297	Oakland Hills CC, Birmingham, MI
1925	*W. MacFarlane	291	Worcester CC, Worcester, MA
1926	Robert T. Jones, Jr.	293	Scioto CC, Columbus, OH
1927	*Tommy Armour	301	Oakmont CC, Oakmont, PA
1928	*Johnny Farrell	294	Olympia Fields CC, Matteson, IL
1929	*R. T. Jones, Jr.	294	Winged Foot GC, Marmaroneck, NY
1930	Robert T. Jones, Jr.	287	Interlachen CC, Hopkins, MN
1931	*Billy Burke	282	Inverness Club, Toledo, OH
1932	Gene Sarazen	286	Fresh Meadows CC, Flushing, NY
1933	Johnny Goodman	287	North Shore CC, Glenview, IL
1934	Olin Dutra	293	Merion Cricket Club, Ardmore, PA
1935	Sam Parks, Jr.	299	Oakmont CC, Oakmont, PA
1936	Tony Manero	282	Baltusrol GC, Springfield, NJ
1937	Ralph Guldahl	281	Oakland Hills CC, Birmingham, MI
1938	Ralph Guldahl	284	Cherry Hills CC, Denver, CO
1939	*Byron Nelson	284	Philadelphia CC, Philadelphia, PA
1940	*Lawson Little	287	Canterbury GC, Cleveland, OH
1941	Craig Wood	284	Colonial Club, Fort Worth, TX
1942–45	No championships played — Second World War		
1946	*Lloyd Mangrum	284	Canterbury GC, Cleveland, OH
1947	*Lew Worsham	282	St. Louis CC, Clayton, MO
1948	Ben Hogan	276	Riviera CC, Los Angeles, CA
1949	Cary Middlecoff	286	Medinah CC, Medinah, IL
1950	*Ben Hogan	287	Merion Golf Club, Ardmore, PA
1951	Ben Hogan	287	Oakland Hills CC, Birmingham, MI
1952	Julius Boros	281	Northwood CC, Dallas, TX
1953	Ben Hogan	283	Oakmont CC, Oakmont, PA
1954	Ed Furgol	284	Baltusrol GC, Springfield, NJ
1955	*Jack Fleck	287	Olympic Club, San Francisco, CA
1956	Cary Middlecoff	281	Oak Hill CC, Rochester, NY
1957	*Dick Mayer	282	Inverness Club, Toledo, OH
1958	Tommy Bolt	283	Southern Hills CC, Tulsa, OK

United States Open Championship (cont'd.)

Year	Winner	Score	Location
1959	Billy Casper	282	Winged Foot GC, Mamaroneck, NY
1960	Arnold Palmer	280	Cherry Hills CC, Denver, CO
1961	Gene Littler	281	Oakland Hills CC, Birmingham, MI
1962	*Jack Nicklaus	283	Oakmont CC, Oakmont, PA
1963	*Julius Boros	293	The Country Club, Brookline, MA
1964	Ken Venturi	278	Congressional CC, Bethesda, MD
1965	*Gary Player	282	Bellerive CC, St. Louis, MO
1966	*Billy Casper	278	Olympic Club, San Francisco, CA
1967	Jack Nicklaus	275	Baltusrol GC, Springfield, NJ
1968	Lee Trevino	275	Oak Hill CC, Rochester, NY
1969	Orville Moody	281	Champions GC, Houston, TX
1970	Tony Jacklin	281	Hazeltine GC, Chaska, MN
1971	*Lee Trevino	280	Merion GC, Ardmore, PA
1972	Jack Nicklaus	290	Pebble Beach GL, Pebble Beach, CA
1973	Johnny Miller	279	Oakmont CC, Oakmont, PA
1974	Hale Irwin	287	Winged Foot GC, Mamaroneck, NY
1975	*Lou Graham	287	Medinah CC, Medinah, IL
1976	Jerry Pate	277	Atlanta Athletic Club, Duluth, GA
1977	Hubert Green	278	Southern Hills CC, Tulsa, OK
1978	Andy North	285	Cherry Hills CC, Denver, CO
1979	Hale Irwin	284	Inverness Club, Toledo, OH
1980	Jack Nicklaus	272	Baltusrol GC, Springfield, NJ
1981	David Graham	273	Merion GC, Ardmore, PA
1982	Tom Watson	282	Pebble Beach GL, Pebble Beach, CA
1983	Larry Nelson	280	Oakmont CC, Oakmont, PA
1984	*Fuzzy Zoeller	276	Winged Foot GC, Mamaroneck, NY
1985	Andy North	279	Oakland Hills CC, Birmingham, MI
1986	Ray Floyd	279	Shinnecock Hills GC, Southampton, NY
1987	Scott Simpson	277	Olympic Club Lake Course, San Francisco, CA
1988	*Curtis Strange	278	The Country Club, Brookline, MA
1989	Curtis Strange	278	Oak Hill CC, Rochester, NY
1990	Hale Irwin	280	Medinah CC, Medinah, IL
1991	Payne Stewart	282	Hazeltine GC, Chaska, MN

*Winner in playoff.

British Open

Year	Winner	Score	Location
1860	Willie Park	174	Prestwick, Scotland
(The first event was open only to professional golfers)			
1861	Tom Morris, Sr.,	163	Prestwick, Scotland
(The second annual open was open to amateurs also)			
1862	Tom Morris, Sr.	163	Prestwick, Scotland
1863	Willie Park	168	Prestwick, Scotland
1864	Tom Morris, Sr.	160	Prestwick, Scotland
1865	Andrew Strath	162	Prestwick, Scotland
1866	Willie Park	169	Prestwick, Scotland
1867	Tom Morris, Sr.	170	Prestwick, Scotland
1868	Tom Morris, Jr.	154	Prestwick, Scotland
1869	Tom Morris, Jr.	157	Prestwick, Scotland
1870	Tom Morris, Jr.	149	Prestwick, Scotland
1871	No championship played		
1872	Tom Morris, Jr.	166	Prestwick, Scotland
1873	Tom Kidd	179	St. Andrews, Scotland
1874	Mungo Park	159	Musselburgh, Scotland
1875	Willie Park	166	Prestwick, Scotland
1876	Bob Martin	176	St. Andrews, Scotland
1877	Jamie Anderson	160	Musselburgh, Scotland
1878	Jamie Anderson	157	Prestwick, Scotland
1879	Jamie Anderson	169	St. Andrews, Scotland
1880	Robert Ferguson	162	Musselburgh, Scotland
1881	Robert Ferguson	170	Prestwick, Scotland
1882	Robert Ferguson	171	St. Andrews, Scotland
1883	*Willie Fernie	159	Musselburgh, Scotland
1884	Jack Simpson	160	Prestwick, Scotland
1885	Bob Martin	171	St. Andrews, Scotland
1886	David Brown	157	Musselburgh, Scotland
1887	Willie Park, Jr.	161	Prestwick, Scotland
1888	Jack Burns	171	St. Andrews, Scotland
1889	*Willie Park, Jr.	155	Musselburgh, Scotland
1890	John Ball	164	Prestwick, Scotland
1891	Hugh Kirkaldy	166	St. Andrews, Scotland
(Championship extended from 36 to 72 holes)			
1892	Harold H. Hilton	305	Muirfield, Scotland
1893	William Auchterlonie	322	Prestwick, Scotland
1894	John H. Taylor	326	Royal St. George's, England
1895	John H. Taylor	322	St. Andrews, Scotland
1896	*Harry Vardon	316	Muirfield, Scotland
1897	Harold H. Hilton	314	Hoylake, England
1898	Harry Vardon	307	Prestwick, Scotland
1899	Harry Vardon	310	Royal St. George's, England
1900	John H. Taylor	309	St. Andrews, Scotland
1901	James Braid	309	Muirfield, Scotland
1902	Alexander Herd	307	Hoylake, England
1903	Harry Vardon	300	Prestwick, Scotland
1904	Jack White	296	Royal St. George's, England
1905	James Braid	318	St. Andrews, Scotland
1906	James Braid	300	Muirfield, Scotland
1907	Arnaud Massy	312	Hoylake, England
1908	James Braid	291	Prestwick, Scotland
1909	John H. Taylor	295	Deal, England
1910	James Braid	299	St. Andrews, Scotland
1911	Harry Vardon	303	Royal St. George's, England
1912	Edward (Ted) Ray	295	Muirfield, Scotland
1913	John H. Taylor	304	Hoylake, England
1914	Harry Vardon	306	Prestwick, Scotland
1915–19	No championships played — First World War		
1920	George Duncan	303	Deal, England
1921	*Jock Hutchison	296	St. Andrews, Scotland
1922	Walter Hagen	300	Royal St. George's, England
1923	Arthur G. Havers	295	Troon, Scotland
1924	Walter Hagen	301	Hoylake, England
1925	James M. Barnes	300	Prestwick, Scotland
1926	Robert T. Jones, Jr.	291	Royal Lytham, England
1927	Robert T. Jones, Jr.	285	St. Andrews, Scotland
1928	Walter Hagen	292	Royal St. George's, England
1929	Walter Hagen	292	Muirfield, Scotland
1930	Robert T. Jones, Jr.	291	Hoylake, England
1931	Tommy D. Armour	296	Carnoustie, Scotland
1932	Gene Sarazen	283	Prince's, England
1933	*Denny Shute	292	St. Andrews, Scotland
1934	Henry Cotton	283	Royal St. George's, England
1935	Alfred Perry	283	Muirfield, Scotland
1936	Alfred Padgham	287	Hoylake, England
1937	Henry Cotton	290	Carnoustie, Scotland
1938	R. A. Whitcombe	295	Royal St. George's, England
1939	Richard Burton	290	St. Andrews, Scotland
1940–45	No championships played — Second World War		
1946	Sam Snead	290	St. Andrews, Scotland
1947	Fred Daly	293	Hoylake, England
1948	Henry Cotton	294	Muirfield, Scotland
1949	*Bobby Locke	283	Royal St. George's, England

Year	Winner	Score	Location
1950	Bobby Locke	279	Troon, Scotland
1951	Max Faulkner	285	Portrush, Ireland
1952	Bobby Locke	287	Royal Lytham, England
1953	Ben Hogan	282	Carnoustie, Scotland
1954	Peter Thomson	283	Royal Birkdale, England
1955	Peter Thomson	281	St. Andrews, Scotland
1956	Peter Thomson	286	Hoylake, England
1957	Bobby Locke	279	St. Andrews, Scotland
1958	*Peter Thomson	278	Royal Lytham, England
1959	Gary Player	284	Muirfield, Scotland
1960	Kel Nagle	278	St. Andrews, Scotland
1961	Arnold Palmer	284	Royal Birkdale, England
1962	Arnold Palmer	276	Troon, Scotland
1963	*Bob Charles	277	Royal Lytham, England
1964	Tony Lema	279	St. Andrews, Scotland
1965	Peter Thomson	285	Southport, England
1966	Jack Nicklaus	282	Muirfield, Scotland
1967	Roberto De Vicenzo	278	Hoylake, England
1968	Gary Player	289	Carnoustie, Scotland
1969	Tony Jacklin	280	Royal Lytham, England
1970	*Jack Nicklaus	283	St. Andrews, Scotland
1971	Lee Trevino	278	Royal Birkdale, England
1972	Lee Trevino	278	Muirfield, Scotland
1973	Tom Weiskopf	276	Troon, Scotland
1974	Gary Player	282	Royal Lytham, England
1975	*Tom Watson	279	Carnoustie, Scotland
1976	Johnny Miller	279	Royal Birkdale, England
1977	Tom Watson	268	Turnberry, Scotland
1978	Jack Nicklaus	281	St. Andrews, Scotland
1979	Seve Ballesteros	283	Royal Lytham, England
1980	Tom Watson	271	Muirfield, Scotland
1981	Bill Rogers	276	Royal St. George's, England
1982	Tom Watson	284	Royal Troon, Scotland
1983	Tom Watson	275	Royal Birkdale, England
1984	Seve Ballesteros	276	St. Andrews, Scotland
1985	Sandy Lyle	282	Royal St. George's, England
1986	Greg Norman	280	Turnberry, Scotland
1987	Nick Faldo	279	Muirfield, Scotland
1988	Seve Ballesteros	273	Royal Lytham and St. Annes, England
1989	*Mark Calcavecchia	275	Troon, Scotland
1990	Nick Faldo	270	St. Andrews, Scotland
1991	Ian Baker-Finch	272	Royal Birkdale, England

Winner in playoff.

PGA Championship

Year	Winner	Score	Runner-up	Location
1916	James M. Barnes	1 up	Jock Hutchison	Siwanoy CC, Bronxville, NY
1917–18	*No championships played — First World War*			
1919	James M. Barnes	6 & 5	Fred McLeod	Engineers CC, Roslyn, NY
1920	Jock Hutchison	1 up	J. Douglas Edgar	Flossmoor CC, Flossmoor, IL
1921	Walter Hagen	3 & 2	James M. Barnes	Inwood CC, Inwood, NY
1922	Gene Sarazen	4 & 3	Emmet French	Oakmont CC, Oakmont, PA
1923	Gene Sarazen	1 up (38)	Walter Hagen	Pelham CC, Pelham, NY
1924	Walter Hagen	2 up	James M. Barnes	French Lick CC, French Lick, IN
1925	Walter Hagen	6 & 5	William Mehlhorn	Olympia Fields, Olympia Fields, IL
1926	Walter Hagen	5 & 3	Leo Diegel	Salisbury GC, Westbury, NY
1927	Walter Hagen	1 up	Joe Turnesa	Cedar Crest CC, Dallas, TX
1928	Leo Diegel	6 & 5	Al Espinosa	Five Farms CC, Baltimore, MD
1929	Leo Diegel	6 & 4	Johnny Farrell	Hillcrest CC, Los Angeles, CA
1930	Tommy Armour	1 up	Gene Sarazen	Fresh Meadow CC, Flushing, NY
1931	Tom Creavy	2 & 1	Denny Shute	Wannamoisett CC, Rumford, RI
1932	Olin Dutra	4 & 3	Frank Walsh	Keller GC, St. Paul, MN
1933	Gene Sarazen	5 & 4	Willie Goggin	Blue Mound CC, Milwaukee, WI
1934	Paul Runyan	1 up (38)	Craig Wood	Park CC, Williamsville, NY
1935	Johnny Revolta	5 & 4	Tommy Armour	Twin Hills CC, Oklahoma City, OK
1936	Denny Shute	3 & 2	Jimmy Thomson	Pinehurst CC, Pinehurst, NC
1937	Denny Shute	1 up (37)	Harold McSpaden	Pittsburgh FC, Aspinwall, PA
1938	Paul Runyan	8 & 7	Sam Snead	Shawnee CC, Shawnee-on-Delaware, PA
1939	Henry Picard	1 up (37)	Byron Nelson	Pomonok CC, Flushing, NY
1940	Byron Nelson	1 up	Sam Snead	Hershey CC, Hershey, PA
1941	Vic Ghezzi	1 up (38)	Byron Nelson	Cherry Hills CC, Denver, CO
1942	Sam Snead	2 & 1	Jim Turnesa	Seaview CC, Atlantic City, NJ
1943	*No championship played — Second World War*			
1944	Bob Hamilton	1 up	Byron Nelson	Manito G. & CC., Spokane, WA
1945	Byron Nelson	4 & 3	Sam Byrd	Morraine CC, Dayton, OH
1946	Ben Hogan	6 & 4	Ed Oliver	Portland GC, Portland, OR
1947	Jim Ferrier	2 & 1	Chick Harbert	Plum Hollow CC, Detroit, MI
1948	Ben Hogan	7 & 6	Mike Turnesa	Norwood Hills CC, St. Louis, MO
1949	Sam Snead	3 & 2	Johnny Palmer	Hermitage CC, Richmond, VA
1950	Chandler Harper	4 & 3	Henry Williams, Jr.	Scioto CC, Columbus, OH
1951	Sam Snead	7 & 6	Walter Burkemo	Oakmont CC, Oakmont, PA
1952	Jim Turnesa	1 up	Chick Harbert	Big Spring CC, Louisville, KY
1953	Walter Burkemo	2 & 1	Felice Torza	Birmingham CC, Birmingham, MI
1954	Chick Harbert	4 & 3	Walter Burkemo	Keller GC, St. Paul, MN
1955	Doug Ford	4 & 3	Cary Middlecoff	Meadowbrook CC, Detroit, MI
1956	Jack Burke	3 & 2	Ted Kroll	Blue Hill CC, Boston, MA
1957	Lionel Hebert	2 & 1	Dow Finsterwald	Miami Valley CC, Dayton, OH

Tournament switched to stroke play.

PGA Championship
(cont'd.)

Year	Winner	Score	Runner-up	Location
1958	Dow Finsterwald	276	Billy Casper	Llanerch CC, Havertown, PA
1959	Bob Rosburg	277	Jerry Barber Doug Sanders	Minneapolis GC, St. Louis Park, MN
1960	Jay Hebert	281	Jim Ferrier	Firestone CC, Akron, OH
1961	*Jerry Barber	277	Don January	Olympia Fields CC, Olympia Fields, IL
1962	Gary Player	278	Bob Goalby	Aronomink GC, Newtown Square, PA
1963	Jack Nicklaus	279	Dave Ragan, Jr.	Dallas Athletic Club, Dallas, TX
1964	Bobby Nichols	271	Jack Nicklaus Arnold Palmer	Columbus CC, Columbus, OH
1965	Dave Marr	280	Billy Casper Jack Nicklaus	Laurel Valley CC, Ligonier, PA
1966	Al Geiberger	280	Dudley Wysong	Firestone CC, Akron, OH
1967	*Don January	281	Don Massengale	Columbine CC, Littleton, CO
1968	Julius Boros	281	Bob Charles Arnold Palmer	Pecan Valley CC, San Antonio, TX
1969	Ray Floyd	276	Gary Player	NCR CC, Dayton, OH
1970	Dave Stockton	279	Arnold Palmer Bob Murphy	Southern Hills CC, Tulsa, OK
1971	Jack Nicklaus	281	Billy Casper	PGA National GC, Palm Beach Gardens, FL
1972	Gary Player	281	Tommy Aaron Jim Jamieson	Oakland Hills CC, Birmingham, MI
1973	Jack Nicklaus	277	Bruce Crampton	Canterbury GC, Cleveland, OH
1974	Lee Trevino	276	Jack Nicklaus	Tanglewood GC, Winston-Salem, NC
1975	Jack Nicklaus	276	Bruce Crampton	Firestone CC, Akron, OH

PGA Championship (cont'd.)

Year	Winner	Score	Runner-up	Location
1976	Dave Stockton	281	Ray Floyd Don January	Congressional CC, Bethesda, MD
1977	*Lanny Wadkins	282	Gene Littler	Pebble Beach GL, Pebble Beach, CA
1978	*John Mahaffey	276	Jerry Pate Tom Watson	Oakmont CC, Oakmont, PA
1979	*David Graham	272	Ben Crenshaw	Oakland Hills CC, Birmingham, MI
1980	Jack Nicklaus	274	Andy Bean	Oak Hill CC, Rochester, NY
1981	Larry Nelson	273	Fuzzy Zoeller	Atlanta Athletic Club, Duluth, GA
1982	Raymond Floyd	272	Lanny Wadkins	Southern Hills CC, Tulsa, OK
1983	Hal Sutton	274	Jack Nicklaus	Riviera CC, Pacific Palisades, CA
1984	Lee Trevino	273	Gary Player Lanny Wadkins	Shoal Creek, Birmingham, AL
1985	Hubert Green	278	Lee Trevino	Cherry Hills CC, Denver, CO
1986	Bob Tway	276	Greg Norman	Inverness Club, Toledo, OH
1987	*Larry Nelson	287	Lanny Wadkins	PGA National, Palm Beach Gardens, FL
1988	Jeff Sluman	272	Paul Azinger	Oak Tree GC, Edmond, OK
1989	Payne Stewart	276	Mike Reid	Kemper Lakes GC, Hawthorn Woods, IL
1990	Wayne Grady	282	Fred Couples	Shoal Creek, Birmingham, AL
1991	John Daly	276	B. Lietzke	Crooked Stick GC, Carmel, IN

*Winner in playoff.

Canadian Open

Year	Winner	Score	Location
1904	J. H. Oke	156	Royal Montreal GC, Montreal, PQ
1905	George Cumming	148	Toronto GC, Toronto, ON
1906	Charles Murray	170	Royal Ottawa GC, Ottawa, ON
1907	Percy Barrett	306	Lambton GC, Toronto, ON
1908	Albert Murray	300	Royal Montreal GC, Montreal, PQ
1909	Karl Keffer	309	Toronto GC, Toronto, ON
1910	Daniel Kenny	303	Lambton GC, Toronto, ON
1911	Charles Murray	314	Royal Ottawa GC, Ottawa, ON
1912	George Sargent	299	Rosedale GC, Toronto, ON
1913	Albert Murray	295	Royal Montreal GC, Montreal, PQ
1914	Karl Keffer	300	Toronto GC, Toronto, ON
1915–18	No tournaments — First World War		
1919	J. Douglas Edgar	278	Hamilton GC, Hamilton, ON
1920	*J. Douglas Edgar	298	Rivermead GC, Ottawa, ON
1921	W. H. Trovinger	293	Toronto GC, Toronto, ON
1922	Al Watrous	303	Mt. Bruno GC, Montreal, PQ
1923	C. W. Hackney	295	Lakeview GC, Toronto, ON
1924	Leo Diegel	285	Mt. Bruno GC, Montreal, PQ
1925	Leo Diegel	295	Lambton GC, Toronto, ON
1926	Mac Smith	283	Royal Montreal GC, Montreal, PQ
1927	T. D. Armour	288	Toronto GC, Toronto, ON
1928	Leo Diegel	282	Rosedale GC, Toronto, ON
1929	Leo Diegel	274	Kanawaki GC, Montreal, PQ
1930	*T.D. Armour	273	Hamilton GC, Hamilton, ON
1931	*Walter Hagen	292	Mississauga G & CC, Mississauga, ON
1932	Harry Cooper	290	Ottawa Hunt Club, Ottawa, ON
1933	Joe Kirkwood	282	Royal York GC, Toronto, ON
1934	T. D. Armour	287	Lakeview GC, Toronto, ON
1935	Gene Kunes	280	Summerlea GC, Montreal, PQ

Canadian Open
(cont'd.)

Year	Winner	Score	Location
1936	Lawson Little	271	St. Andrews GC, Toronto, ON
1937	Harry Cooper	285	St. Andrews GC, Toronto, ON
1938	*Sam Snead	277	Mississauga G & CC, Mississauga, ON
1939	H. McSpaden	282	Riverside GC, Saint John, NB
1940	*Sam Snead	281	Scarborough G & CC, Toronto, ON
1941	Sam Snead	274	Lambton GC, Toronto, ON
1942	Craig Wood	275	Mississauga G & CC, Mississauga, ON
1943–44	*No tournaments — Second World War*		
1945	Byron Nelson	280	Thornhill GC, Toronto, ON
1946	*George Fazio	278	Beaconsfield GC, Montreal, PQ
1947	Bobby Locke	268	Scarborough G & CC, Toronto, ON
1948	C. W. Congdon	280	Shaughnessy Heights GC, Vancouver, BC
1949	E.J. "Dutch" Harrison	271	St. Georges G & CC, Toronto, ON
1950	Jim Ferrier	271	Royal Montreal GC, Montreal, PQ
1951	Jim Ferrier	273	Mississauga G & CC, Mississauga, ON
1952	John Palmer	263	St. Charles CC, Winnipeg, MN
1953	Dave Douglas	273	Scarborough G & CC, Toronto, ON
1954	Pat Fletcher	280	Point Grey GC, Vancouver, BC
1955	Arnold Palmer	265	Weston GC, Toronto, ON
1956	#Doug Sanders	273	Beaconsfield GC, Montreal, PQ
1957	George Bayer	271	Westmount G & CC, Kitchener, ON
1958	Wesley Ellis, Jr.	267	Mayfair G & CC, Edmonton, AL
1959	Doug Ford	276	Islesmere G & CC, Montreal, PQ
1960	Art Wall, Jr.	269	St. Georges G & CC, Toronto, ON
1961	Jacky Cupit	270	Niakwa GC, Winnipeg, MN
1962	Ted Kroll	278	Laval sur-le-Lac, Montreal, PQ
1963	Doug Ford	280	Scarborough G & CC, Toronto, ON
1964	Nel Nagle	277	Finegrove CC, St. Luc, PQ
1965	Gene Littler	273	Mississauga G & CC, Mississauga, ON
1966	D. Massengale	280	Shaughnessy G & CC, Toronto, ON
1967	*Billy Casper	279	Montreal Municipal GC, Montreal, PQ
1968	Bob Charles	274	St. Georges G & CC, Toronto, ON
1969	*Tommy Aaron	275	Pinegrove G & CC, St. Luc, PQ
1970	Kermit Zarley	279	London Hunt & CC, London, ON
1971	*Lee Trevino	275	Richelieu Valley GC, Montreal, PQ
1972	Gay Brewer	275	Cherry Hill Club, Ridgeway, ON
1973	Tom Weiskopf	278	Richelieu Valley G & CC, Ste. Julie de Verchères, PQ
1974	Bobby Nichols	270	Mississauga G & CC, Mississauga, ON
1975	*Tom Weiskopf	274	Royal Montreal GC, Ile Bizard, PQ
1976	Jerry Pate	267	Essex G & CC, Windsor, ON
1977	Lee Trevino	280	Glen Abbey GC, Oakville, ON
1978	Bruce Lietzke	283	Glen Abbey GC, Oakville, ON
1979	Lee Trevino	281	Glen Abbey GC, Oakville, ON
1980	Bob Gilder	274	Royal Montreal GC, Ile Bizard, PQ
1981	Peter Oosterhuis	280	Glen Abbey GC, Oakville, ON
1982	Bruce Lietzke	277	Glen Abbey GC, Oakville, ON
1983	*John Cook	277	Glen Abbey GC, Oakville, ON
1984	Greg Norman	278	Glen Abbey GC, Oakville, ON
1985	Curtis Strange	279	Glen Abbey GC, Oakville, ON
1986	Bob Murphy	280	Glen Abbey GC, Oakville, ON
1987	Curtis Strange	276	Glen Abbey GC, Oakville, ON
1988	Ken Green	275	Glen Abbey GC, Oakville, ON
1989	Steve Jones	271	Glen Abbey GC, Oakville, ON
1990	Wayne Levi	278	Glen Abbey GC, Oakville, ON
1991	Nick Price	273	Glen Abbey GC, Oakville, ON

*Winner in playoff

#Amateur

Ryder Cup

Year	Winner				Location
1927	U.S.	9½	Britain	2½	Worcester Country Club, Worcester, MA
1929	Britain	7	U.S.	5	Moortown, England
1931	U.S.	9	Britain	3	Scioto Country Club, Columbus, OH
1933	Britain	6½	U.S.	5½	Southport & Ainsdale Courses, England
1935	U.S.	9	Britain	3	Ridgewood Country Club, Ridgewood, NJ
1937	U.S.	8	Britain	4	Southport & Ainsdale Courses, England

Ryder Cup matches not held during Second World War years.

Year	Winner				Location
1947	U.S.	11	Britain	1	Portland Golf Club, Portland, OR
1949	U.S.	7	Britain	5	Ganton Golf Course, Scarborough, England
1951	U.S.	9½	Britain	2½	Pinehurst Country Club, Pinehurst, NC
1953	U.S.	6½	Britain	5½	Wentworth, England
1955	U.S.	8	Britain	4	Thunderbird Ranch and Country Club, Palm Springs, CA
1957	Britain	7½	U.S.	4½	Lindrick Golf Club, Yorkshire, England
1959	U.S.	8½	Britain	3½	Eldorado Country Club, Palm Desert, CA
1961	U.S.	14½	Britain	9½	Royal Lytham and St. Annes Golf Club, St. Anne's-On-The-Sea, England
1963	U.S.	23	Britain	9	East Lake Country Club, Atlanta, GA
1965	U.S.	19½	Britain	12½	Royal Birkdale Golf Club, Southport, England
1967	U.S.	23½	Britain	8½	Champions Golf Club, Houston, TX
1969	U.S.	16	Britain	16 (Tie)	Royal Birkdale Golf Club, Southport, England
1971	U.S.	18½	Britain	13½	Old Warson Country Club, St. Louis, MO
1973	U.S.	19	Britain	13	Muirfield, Scotland
1975	U.S.	21	Britain	11	Laurel Valley Golf Club, Ligonier, PA
1977	U.S.	12½	Britain	7½	Royal Lytham and St. Annes Golf Club, St. Anne's-On-The-Sea, England
1979	U.S.	17	Europe	11	The Greenbrier, White Sulphur Springs, WV
1981	U.S.	18½	Europe	9½	Walton Heath Golf Club, Surrey, England
1983	U.S.	14½	Europe	13½	PGA National GC, Palm Beach Gardens, FL
1985	Europe	16½	U.S.	11½	The Belfry Golf Club, Sutton Coldfield, England
1987	Europe	15	U.S.	13	Muirfield Village Golf Club, Dublin, OH
1989	Europe	14	U.S.	14	The Belfry Golf Club, Sutton Coldfield, England
1991	U.S.	14½	Europe	13½	The Ocean Course, Kiawah Island, SC

In case of tie, previous winner retains Cup.

U.S. Women's Open

Year	Winner	Score	Location
1946	Patty Berg	5&4	Spokane CC, Spokane, WA
1947	Betty Jameson	295	Starmount Forest CC, Greensboro, NC
1948	Babe Zaharias	300	Atlantic City CC, Northfield, NJ
1949	Louise Suggs	291	Prince Georges CC, Landover, MD
1950	Babe Zaharias	291	Rolling Hills CC, Wichita, KS
1951	Betsy Rawls	293	Druid Hills GC, Atlanta, GA
1952	Louise Suggs	284	Bala GC, Philadelphia, PA
1953	*Betsy Rawls	302	CC of Rochester, Rochester, NY
1954	Babe Zaharias	291	Salem CC, Peabody, MA
1955	Fay Crocker	299	Wichita CC, Wichita, KS
1956	*Kathy Cornelius	302	Northland CC, Duluth, MN
1957	Betsy Rawls	299	Winged Foot GC, Mamaroneck, NY
1958	Mickey Wright	290	Forest Lake CC, Detroit, MI
1959	Mickey Wright	287	Churchill Valley CC, Pittsburgh, PA
1960	Betsy Rawls	292	Worcester CC, Worcester, MA
1961	Mickey Wright	293	Baltusrol GC, Springfield, NJ
1962	Murle Breer	301	Dunes GC, Myrtle Beach, SC
1963	Mary Mills	289	Kenwood CC, Cincinnati, OH
1964	*Mickey Wright	290	San Diego CC, Chula Vista, CA
1965	Carol Mann	290	Atlantic City CC, Northfield, NJ
1966	Sandra Spuzich	297	Hazeltine National GC, Chaska, MN
1967	#Catherine LaCoste	294	Hot Springs GC, Hot Springs, VA
1968	Susie Berning	289	Moselem Springs GC, Fleetwood, PA
1969	Donna Caponi	294	Scenic Hills CC, Pensacola, FL
1970	Donna Caponi	287	Muskogee CC, Muskogee, OK
1971	JoAnne Carner	288	Kahkwa CC, Erie, PA
1972	Susie Berning	299	Winged Foot GC, Mamaroneck, NY
1973	Susie Berning	290	CC of Rochester, Rochester, NY
1974	Sandra Haynie	295	La Grange CC, La Grange, IL
1975	Sandra Palmer	295	Atlantic City CC, Northfield, NJ
1976	*JoAnne Carner	292	Rolling Green CC, Springfield, PA
1977	Hollis Stacy	292	Hazeltine National GC, Chaska, MN
1978	Hollis Stacy	289	CC of Indianapolis, Indianapolis, IN
1979	Jerilyn Britz	284	Brooklawn CC, Fairfield, CT
1980	Amy Alcott	280	Richland CC, Nashville, TN
1981	Pat Bradley	279	La Grange CC, La Grange, IL
1982	Janet Anderson	283	Del Paso CC, Sacramento, CA
1983	Jan Stephenson	290	Cedar Ridge CC, Tulsa, OK
1984	Hollis Stacy	290	Salem CC, Peabody, MA
1985	Kathy Baker	280	Baltusrol GC, Springfield, NJ
1986	*Jane Geddes	287	NCR GC, Dayton, OH
1987	*Laura Davies	285	Plainfield CC, Plainfield, NJ
1988	Liselotte Neumann	277	Baltimore CC, Baltimore, MD
1989	Betsy King	278	Indian Wood G&CC, Lake Orion, MI
1990	Betsy King	284	Atlanta Athletic Club, Duluth, GA
1991	Meg Mallon	283	Colonial CC, Ft. Worth, TX

*Winner in playoff
#Amateur

U.S. Senior Open

Year	Winner	Score	Location
1980	Roberto De Vicenzo	285	Winged Foot GC (East), Mamaroneck, NY
1981	*Arnold Palmer	289	Oakland Hills CC, Birmingham, MI
1982	Miller Barber	282	Portland GC, Portland, OR
1983	*Billy Casper	288	Hazeltine National GC, Chaska, MN
1984	Miller Barber	286	Oak Hill CC, Rochester, NY
1985	Miller Barber	285	Edgewood Tahoe GC, Stateline, NV
1986	Dale Douglass	279	Scioto CC, Columbus, OH
1987	Gary Player	270	Brooklawn CC, Fairfield, CT
1988	*Gary Player	288	Medinah CC, Medinah, IL
1989	Orville Moody	279	Laurel Valley CC, Ligonier, PA
1990	Lee Trevino	275	Ridgewood CC, Paramus, NJ
1991	*Jack Nicklaus	282	Oakland Hills CC, Birmingham, MI

*Winner in playoff

Australian Open

Year	Winner	Score	Location
1904	#M. Scott	315	The Australian, Sydney, NSW
1905	D. Soutar	337	Royal Melbourne, Melbourne, VIC
1906	C. Clark	322	Royal Sydney, Sydney, NSW
1907	#M. Scott	318	Royal Melbourne, Melbourne, VIC
1908	#C. Pearce	311	The Australian, Sydney, NSW
1909	#C. Felstead	316	Royal Melbourne, Melbourne, VIC
1910	C. Clark	306	Seaton, Seaton, VIC
1911	C. Clark	321	Royal Sydney, Sydney, NSW
1912	#I. Whitton	321	Royal Melbourne, Melbourne, VIC
1913	#I. Whitton	302	Royal Melbourne, Melbourne, VIC
1914–19	*Championship not played — First World War*		
1920	J. Kirkwood	290	The Australian, Sydney, NSW
1921	A. Le Fevre	295	Royal Melbourne, Melbourne, VIC
1922	C. Campbell	307	Royal Sydney, Sydney, NSW
1923	T. Howard	301	Royal Adelaide, Adelaide, SA
1924	#A. Russell	303	Royal Melbourne, Melbourne, VIC
1925	F. Popplewell	299	The Australian, Sydney, NSW
1926	#I. Whitton	297	Royal Adelaide, Adelaide, SA
1927	R. Stewart	297	Royal Melbourne, Melbourne, VIC
1928	F. Popplewell	295	Royal Sydney, Sydney, NSW
1929	#I. Whitton	309	Royal Adelaide, Adelaide, SA
1930	F. Eyre	306	Metropolitan, Oakleigh, VIC
1931	#I. Whitton	301	The Australian, Sydney, NSW
1932	#M. Ryan	296	Royal Adelaide, Adelaide, SA
1933	M.L. Kelly	302	Royal Melbourne, Melbourne, VIC
1934	W. Bolger	283	Royal Sydney, Sydney, NSW
1935	F. McMahon	293	Royal Adelaide, Adelaide, SA
1936	G. Sarazen	282	Metropolitan, Oakleigh, VIC
1937	G. Naismith	299	The Australian, Sydney, NSW
1938	#J. Ferrier	283	Royal Adelaide, Adelaide, SA
1939	#J. Ferrier	285	Royal Melbourne, Melbourne, VIC
1940–45	*Championship not played — Second World War*		
1946	O. Pickworth	289	Royal Sydney, Sydney, NSW
1947	O. Pickworth	285	Royal Queensland, Hamilton, VIC
1948	*O. Pickworth	289	Kingston Heath, Melbourne, VIC
1949	E. Cremin	287	The Australian, Sydney, NSW
1950	N. von Nida	286	Kooyonga, Adelaide, SA
1951	P. Thomson	283	Metropolitan, Oakleigh, VIC
1952	N. von Nida	278	Lake Karrinyup, Balcatta, NA
1953	N. von Nida	278	Royal Melbourne, Melbourne, VIC

Australian Open (cont'd.)

Year	Winner	Score	Location
1954	O. Pickworth	280	Kooyonga, Adelaide, SA
1955	A.D. Locke	290	Gailes, Brisbane, QLD
1956	B. Crampton	289	Royal Sydney, Sydney, NSW
1957	F. Phillips	287	Kingston Heath, Melbourne, VIC
1958	G. Player	271	Kooyonga, Adelaide, SA
1959	K. Nagle	284	The Australian, Sydney, NSW
1960	#B. Devlin	282	Lake Karrinyup, Balcatta, NA
1961	F. Phillips	275	Victoria, Melbourne, VIC
1962	G. Player	281	Royal Adelaide, Adelaide, SA
1963	G. Player	278	Royal Melbourne, Melbourne, VIC
1964	*J. Nicklaus	287	The Lakes, Sydney, NSW
1965	G. Player	264	Kooyonga, Adelaide, SA
1966	A. Palmer	276	Royal Queensland, Hamilton, VIC
1967	P. Thomson	281	Commonwealth, Melbourne, VIC
1968	J. Nicklaus	270	Lake Karrinyup, Balcatta, NA
1969	G. Player	288	Royal Sydney, Sydney, NSW
1970	G. Player	280	Kingston Heath, Melbourne, VIC
1971	J. Nicklaus	269	Royal Hobart, Hobart, TAS
1972	*P. Thomson	281	Kooyonga, Adelaide, SA
1973	J.C. Snead	280	Royal Queensland, Hamilton, VIC
1974	G. Player	277	Lake Karrinyup, Balcatta, NA
1975	J. Nicklaus	279	The Australian, Sydney, NSW
1976	J. Nicklaus	286	The Australian, Sydney, NSW
1977	D. Graham	284	The Australian, Sydney, NSW
1978	J. Nicklaus	284	The Australian, Sydney, NSW
1979	J. Newton	288	Metropolitan, Oakleigh, VIC
1980	G. Norman	284	The Lakes, Sydney, NSW
1981	W. Rogers	282	Victoria, Melbourne, VIC
1982	R. Shearer	287	The Australian, Sydney, NSW
1983	P. Fowler	285	Kingston Heath, Melbourne, VIC
1984	T. Watson	281	Royal Melbourne, Melbourne, VIC
1985	G. Norman	212	Royal Melbourne, Melbourne, VIC
1986	R. Davis	278	Metropolitan, Oakleigh, VIC
1987	G. Norman	273	Royal Melbourne, Melbourne, VIC
1988	M. Calcavecchia	269	Royal Sydney, Sydney, NSW
1989	P. Senior	271	Kingston Heath, Melbourne, VIC
1990	*J. Morse	283	The Australian, Sydney, NSW

*Winner in playoff
#Amateur

Personal
Rounds

VI ET ARTE

DATE: _____

COURSE: _____

CONDITIONS: _____

PLAYING PARTNERS: A) _____

B) _____

C) _____

SCORES:

Hole	Par	Self	A	B	C	Comments
1						
2						
3						
4						
5						
6						
7						
8						
9						
OUT						
10						
11						
12						
13						
14						
15						
16						
17						
18						
IN						
TOTAL						

DATE: _____

COURSE: _____

CONDITIONS: _____

PLAYING PARTNERS: A) _____

B) _____

C) _____

SCORES:

Hole	Par	Self	A	B	C	Comments
1						
2						
3						
4						
5						
6						
7						
8						
9						
OUT						
10						
11						
12						
13						
14						
15						
16						
17						
18						
IN						
TOTAL						

DATE: _____

COURSE: _____

CONDITIONS: _____

PLAYING PARTNERS: A) _____

B) _____

C) _____

SCORES:

Hole	Par	Self	A	B	C	Comments
1						
2						
3						
4						
5						
6						
7						
8						
9						
OUT						
10						
11						
12						
13						
14						
15						
16						
17						
18						
IN						
TOTAL						

DATE: _____

COURSE: _____

CONDITIONS: _____

PLAYING PARTNERS: A) _____

B) _____

C) _____

SCORES:

Hole	Par	Self	A	B	C	Comments
1						
2						
3						
4						
5						
6						
7						
8						
9						
OUT						
10						
11						
12						
13						
14						
15						
16						
17						
18						
IN						
TOTAL						

DATE: _____

COURSE: _____

CONDITIONS: _____

PLAYING PARTNERS: A) _____

B) _____

C) _____

SCORES:

Hole	Par	Self	A	B	C	Comments
1						
2						
3						
4						
5						
6						
7						
8						
9						
OUT						
10						
11						
12						
13						
14						
15						
16						
17						
18						
IN						
TOTAL						

DATE: _____

COURSE: _____

CONDITIONS: _____

PLAYING PARTNERS: A) _____

B) _____

C) _____

SCORES:

Hole	Par	Self	A	B	C	Comments
1						
2						
3						
4						
5						
6						
7						
8						
9						
OUT						
10						
11						
12						
13						
14						
15						
16						
17						
18						
IN						
TOTAL						

DATE: _____

COURSE: _____

CONDITIONS: _____

PLAYING PARTNERS: A) _____

B) _____

C) _____

SCORES:

Hole	Par	Self	A	B	C	Comments
1						
2						
3						
4						
5						
6						
7						
8						
9						
OUT						
10						
11						
12						
13						
14						
15						
16						
17						
18						
IN						
TOTAL						

DATE: _____

COURSE: _____

CONDITIONS: _____

PLAYING PARTNERS: A) _____

B) _____

C) _____

SCORES:

Hole	Par	Self	A	B	C	Comments
1						
2						
3						
4						
5						
6						
7						
8						
9						
OUT						
10						
11						
12						
13						
14						
15						
16						
17						
18						
IN						
TOTAL						

DATE: _____

COURSE: _____

CONDITIONS: _____

PLAYING PARTNERS: A) _____

B) _____

C) _____

SCORES:

Hole	Par	Self	A	B	C	Comments
1						
2						
3						
4						
5						
6						
7						
8						
9						
OUT						
10						
11						
12						
13						
14						
15						
16						
17						
18						
IN						
TOTAL						

DATE: _____

COURSE: _____

CONDITIONS: _____

PLAYING PARTNERS: A) _____

B) _____

C) _____

SCORES:

Hole	Par	Self	A	B	C	Comments
1						
2						
3						
4						
5						
6						
7						
8						
9						
OUT						
10						
11						
12						
13						
14						
15						
16						
17						
18						
IN						
TOTAL						

DATE: _____

COURSE: _____

CONDITIONS: _____

PLAYING PARTNERS: A) _____

B) _____

C) _____

SCORES:

Hole	Par	Self	A	B	C	Comments
1						
2						
3						
4						
5						
6						
7						
8						
9						
OUT						
10						
11						
12						
13						
14						
15						
16						
17						
18						
IN						
TOTAL						

DATE: _____

COURSE: _____

CONDITIONS: _____

PLAYING PARTNERS: A) _____

B) _____

C) _____

SCORES:

Hole	Par	Self	A	B	C	Comments
1						
2						
3						
4						
5						
6						
7						
8						
9						
OUT						
10						
11						
12						
13						
14						
15						
16						
17						
18						
IN						
TOTAL						

DATE: _____

COURSE: _____

CONDITIONS: _____

PLAYING PARTNERS: A) _____

B) _____

C) _____

SCORES:

Hole	Par	Self	A	B	C	Comments
1						
2						
3						
4						
5						
6						
7						
8						
9						
OUT						
10						
11						
12						
13						
14						
15						
16						
17						
18						
IN						
TOTAL						

DATE: _____

COURSE: _____

CONDITIONS: _____

PLAYING PARTNERS: A) _____

B) _____

C) _____

SCORES:

Hole	Par	Self	A	B	C	Comments
1						
2						
3						
4						
5						
6						
7						
8						
9						
OUT						
10						
11						
12						
13						
14						
15						
16						
17						
18						
IN						
TOTAL						

DATE: _____

COURSE: _____

CONDITIONS: _____

PLAYING PARTNERS: A) _____

B) _____

C) _____

SCORES:

Hole	Par	Self	A	B	C	Comments
1						
2						
3						
4						
5						
6						
7						
8						
9						
OUT						
10						
11						
12						
13						
14						
15						
16						
17						
18						
IN						
TOTAL						

DATE: _____

COURSE: _____

CONDITIONS: _____

PLAYING PARTNERS: A) _____

                                       B) _____

                                       C) _____

SCORES:

Hole	Par	Self	A	B	C	Comments
1						
2						
3						
4						
5						
6						
7						
8						
9						
OUT						
10						
11						
12						
13						
14						
15						
16						
17						
18						
IN						
TOTAL						

DATE: _____

COURSE: _____

CONDITIONS: _____

PLAYING PARTNERS: A) _____

　　　　　　　　　　　 B) _____

　　　　　　　　　　　 C) _____

SCORES:

Hole	Par	Self	A	B	C	Comments
1						
2						
3						
4						
5						
6						
7						
8						
9						
OUT						
10						
11						
12						
13						
14						
15						
16						
17						
18						
IN						
TOTAL						

108

DATE: _____

COURSE: _____

CONDITIONS: _____

PLAYING PARTNERS: A) _____

B) _____

C) _____

SCORES:

Hole	Par	Self	A	B	C	Comments
1						
2						
3						
4						
5						
6						
7						
8						
9						
OUT						
10						
11						
12						
13						
14						
15						
16						
17						
18						
IN						
TOTAL						

DATE: _____

COURSE: _____

CONDITIONS: _____

PLAYING PARTNERS: A) _____

B) _____

C) _____

SCORES:

Hole	Par	Self	A	B	C	Comments
1						
2						
3						
4						
5						
6						
7						
8						
9						
OUT						
10						
11						
12						
13						
14						
15						
16						
17						
18						
IN						
TOTAL						

DATE: _____

COURSE: _____

CONDITIONS: _____

PLAYING PARTNERS: A) _____

B) _____

C) _____

SCORES:

Hole	Par	Self	A	B	C	Comments
1						
2						
3						
4						
5						
6						
7						
8						
9						
OUT						
10						
11						
12						
13						
14						
15						
16						
17						
18						
IN						
TOTAL						

DATE: _____

COURSE: _____

CONDITIONS: _____

PLAYING PARTNERS: A) _____

B) _____

C) _____

SCORES:

Hole	Par	Self	A	B	C	Comments
1						
2						
3						
4						
5						
6						
7						
8						
9						
OUT						
10						
11						
12						
13						
14						
15						
16						
17						
18						
IN						
TOTAL						

DATE: _____

COURSE: _____

CONDITIONS: _____

PLAYING PARTNERS: A) _____

B) _____

C) _____

SCORES:

Hole	Par	Self	A	B	C	Comments
1						
2						
3						
4						
5						
6						
7						
8						
9						
OUT						
10						
11						
12						
13						
14						
15						
16						
17						
18						
IN						
TOTAL						

DATE: _____

COURSE: _____

CONDITIONS: _____

PLAYING PARTNERS: A) _____

B) _____

C) _____

SCORES:

Hole	Par	Self	A	B	C	Comments
1						
2						
3						
4						
5						
6						
7						
8						
9						
OUT						
10						
11						
12						
13						
14						
15						
16						
17						
18						
IN						
TOTAL						

DATE: _____

COURSE: _____

CONDITIONS: _____

PLAYING PARTNERS: A) _____

B) _____

C) _____

SCORES:

Hole	Par	Self	A	B	C	Comments
1						
2						
3						
4						
5						
6						
7						
8						
9						
OUT						
10						
11						
12						
13						
14						
15						
16						
17						
18						
IN						
TOTAL						

DATE: _____

COURSE: _____

CONDITIONS: _____

PLAYING PARTNERS: A) _____

B) _____

C) _____

SCORES:

Hole	Par	Self	A	B	C	Comments
1						
2						
3						
4						
5						
6						
7						
8						
9						
OUT						
10						
11						
12						
13						
14						
15						
16						
17						
18						
IN						
TOTAL						

DATE: _____

COURSE: _____

CONDITIONS: _____

PLAYING PARTNERS: A) _____

B) _____

C) _____

SCORES:

Hole	Par	Self	A	B	C	Comments
1						
2						
3						
4						
5						
6						
7						
8						
9						
OUT						
10						
11						
12						
13						
14						
15						
16						
17						
18						
IN						
TOTAL						

DATE: _____

COURSE: _____

CONDITIONS: _____

PLAYING PARTNERS: A) _____

B) _____

C) _____

SCORES:

Hole	Par	Self	A	B	C	Comments
1						
2						
3						
4						
5						
6						
7						
8						
9						
OUT						
10						
11						
12						
13						
14						
15						
16						
17						
18						
IN						
TOTAL						

DATE: _____

COURSE: _____

CONDITIONS: _____

PLAYING PARTNERS: A) _____

B) _____

C) _____

SCORES:

Hole	Par	Self	A	B	C	Comments
1						
2						
3						
4						
5						
6						
7						
8						
9						
OUT						
10						
11						
12						
13						
14						
15						
16						
17						
18						
IN						
TOTAL						

Acknowledgments

The Bettmann Archive, page 38 (bottom)

Michael French, pages 2, 64

Harbour Town Golf Links/Hugh Owen, page 65 (bottom)

Leonard Kamsler, pages 26, 27, 38 (top), 47 (top), 49

John Knight, page 11

The Mansell Collection, page 13 (top)

Brian D. Morgan, pages 10, 34 (top), 39, 43 (top), 45 (bottom), 46 (bottom), 56, 57, 72, 73

James Niblick Golfiana, 19 Tromley Dr., Islington, Ontario, Canada M9B 5Y4, pages 8, 9, 13 (bottom), 14–17, 19, 22–25, 28, 29, 31, 33, 75, 76, 78, 80, 82, 85–90

United States Golf Association, pages 34 (bottom), 35 (bottom), 36 (bottom), 37, 40, 42 (top), 43 (bottom), 44, 45 (top), 46 (top), 47 (bottom)

Fred Vuich, pages 6, 7, 32, 35 (top), 36 (top), 41, 42 (bottom), 48, 65 (top), 84

Wide World Photos, page 21